HOW TO CREATE
BEADED and WIRE
Tree Sculpture

Sal Vill

THIRD EDITION

HOW TO CREATE
BEADED and WIRE
Tree Sculpture

Sal Villano

Copyright 2009
Sal Villano

Printed in The United States of America
Design Group Publishing
PO Box 827
Milford, Ohio 45150
www.salvillano.com
salvillano@gmail.com

No part of this publication may be reproduced, copied, transmitted or stored in any form, without the written permission of the author.

*To
Uncle Charlie*

*For his
Guidance
Encouragement
and
Friendship*

I think that I shall never see
A poem lovely as a tree.

A tree whose hungry mouth is prest
Against the earth's sweet flowing breast;

A tree that looks at God all day,
And lifts her leafy arms to pray;

A tree that may in summer wear
A nest of robins in her hair;

Upon whose bosom snow has lain;
Who intimately lives with rain.

Poems are made by fools like me,
But only God can make a tree.

TREES
by
Joyce Kilmer 1886 - 1918

TABLE OF CONTENTS

Making the wire wrapping jig..1
Wrapping the wire..3
Creating the root system...9
Wiring the trunk and branches..14
Forming the tree...16
Thickening the tree...17
Final Branching..19
Creating the anchors...20
Preparing the tree for mounting..23
Preparing the base...24
Mounting the tree onto the base...27
Creating the root mound..29
Final construction of the root mound..32
Adding color to the root mound...33
The style of tree you wish to create..35
Weeping willow..36
Beaded..41
Wind swept..45
Oak..50
Bonsai with leaves..60
About the artist..67

Before You Start

Before you start this or any other art or craft project be sure you keep safety as a major part of your procedure. Always protect your eyes, lungs, and skin with quality made protection devices.

All the material and tools necessary to create any of the tree sculptures in this book are available from general supply sources, such as: Arts and Crafts stores, Hardware stores, Florist supply companies. If you take this book with you when you are shopping for your supplies you can refer to it and see exactly what is needed. Although I do not recommend or promote any store or company, If you are having difficulty obtaining any material or tool described in this book, please contact me and I will be happy to give you the names and addresses of the suppliers I use. I can be contacted at:

Sal Villano
PO Box 827   Milford, Ohio   45150
Web site: www.salvillano.com
email: salvillano@gmail.com

I would strongly recommend that you read this entire book before you start to create any tree sculpture. This will help you to understand the steps before you start to create your tree sculpture.

When you are selecting the type of wire you wish to use to create your tree sculpture, you should know how the thickness or "gauge" of the wire is indicated. The gauge of the wire is represented by numbers, such as: 26 gauge, 30 gauge, 36 gauge. It very important to understand that the SMALLER THE NUMBER - THE THICKER THE WIRE! For example:

26 gauge wire is THICKER THAN 28 gauge wire!

Getting Started

You should also know about the type of wire you may be using. Wire, in general, may change color through the years, but this color change will not affect the strength of the sculpture. The tree sculptures that are bonded onto bases or into pots using sea sand, pebbles or rocks are for indoor display only. Since the bond is created onto a porous material, a water soluble glue is used. Therefore the sculptures should never be submerged in water, left outdoors, or cleaned in a dishwasher. You can clean and dust your finished work using a damp, soft, lint free, cloth. Or you can use a feather duster for the branches and base. You can also use a hand held steam cleaner. Use the steam cleaner on the lowest setting and do not over wet the base.

Characteristics Of Craft Wire

GOLD .... Gold in color only. Will retain its gold color for several years then it may tarnish to a patina finish. (a patina is a green color coating that forms on copper and brass as it ages) It actually is a very nice effect.

COPPER .... 100% will oxidize slowly and change to a darker copper color or patina into a dark green color.

SILVER .... Steel wire with silver color. Will retain silver color for several years, then turn a pale gray.

RUST .... Non galvanized steel will rust and turn dark brown very quickly.

STEEL .... Galvanized will keep it's color for many years.

BRASS .... Will turn a dark brown brass color, tarnish and patina.

You Can Create 5 Different Wire and Beaded TREE SCULPTURES...

BEADED

WILLOW

WIND SWEPT

BONSAI with LEAVES

OAK

All material and tools needed to create these Tree Sculptures are available through easy to locate sources, such as Craft Stores, Hobby Shops, Hardware Stores, Florists and Nature. This book contains a complete list of everything needed to create 5 VERY DIFFERENT TREE SCULPTURES.

See All My Tree Sculpture at: www.salvillano.com

Making The Wire Wrapping Jig

The word "jig" may be new to you, so I'll explain what it is and what we will use it for. A jig is a devise that is used to aid, speed up or make more exact the construction or assembly of something else. A jig is used to create the same object over and over again to the same standards. However, the jig itself is not part of the final product, but it is an important part of the process to create the final product. For the creation of wire trees, the jig is used to control the size and total amount of wire needed for the basic tree structure you will be creating. After you make your jig, you should save it for future use. The jig can be altered by changing the position of the nails and the amount of wire wraps used to create larger and different varieties of tree sculpture. The jig you will need is very easy to construct using a piece of wood, (it can be scrap wood), cut to the sizes indicated in the illustration plus three 2.5" or 3" finishing nails. Finishing nails are nail that have small heads. The small heads of the nails will help when you need to slip the wire off the nails. *fig.1.*

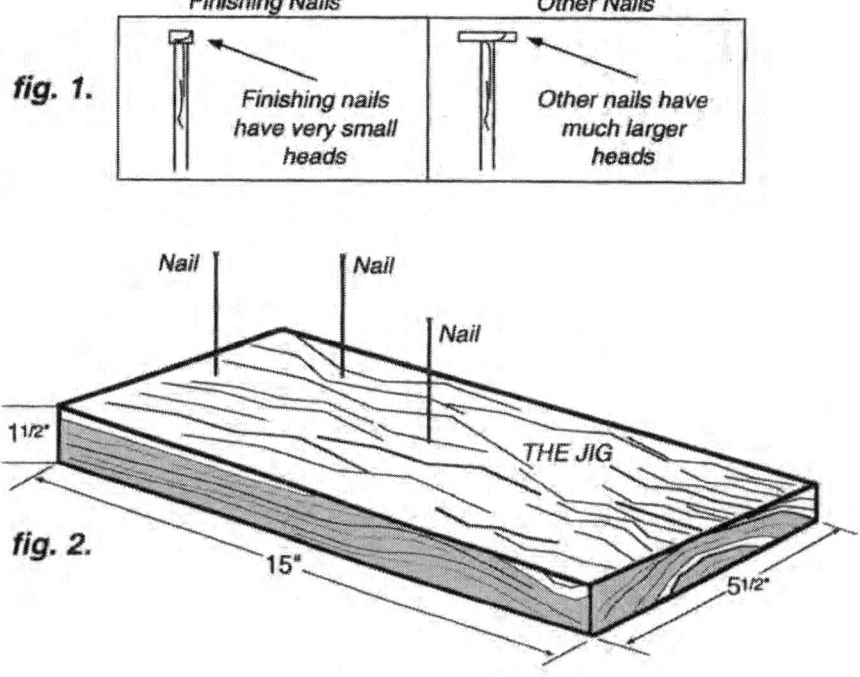

a)
After cutting the wood for the jig to the proper size, sand the edges to eliminate the possibility of splinters. *fig. 2.* Next, draw pencil lines on the wood to the measurements indicated in *fig. 3.* Draw small dots to indicate where you will position the three finishing nails.

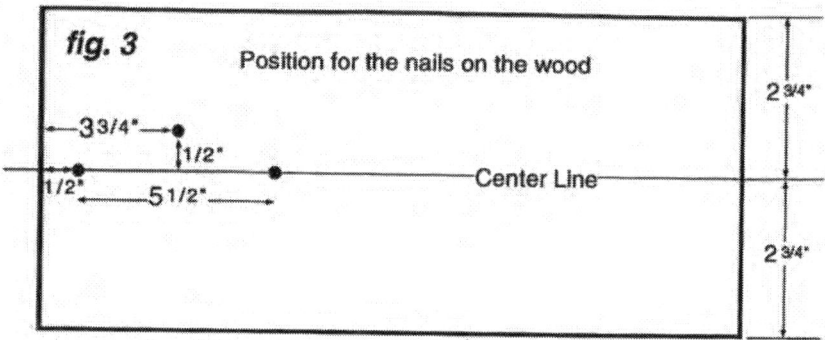

b)
Measure 1/2" up from the point on each of the three finishing nails and mark this spot on the nail in pencil. This will indicate how far into the wood you will need to drive each nail. *fig. 4.*

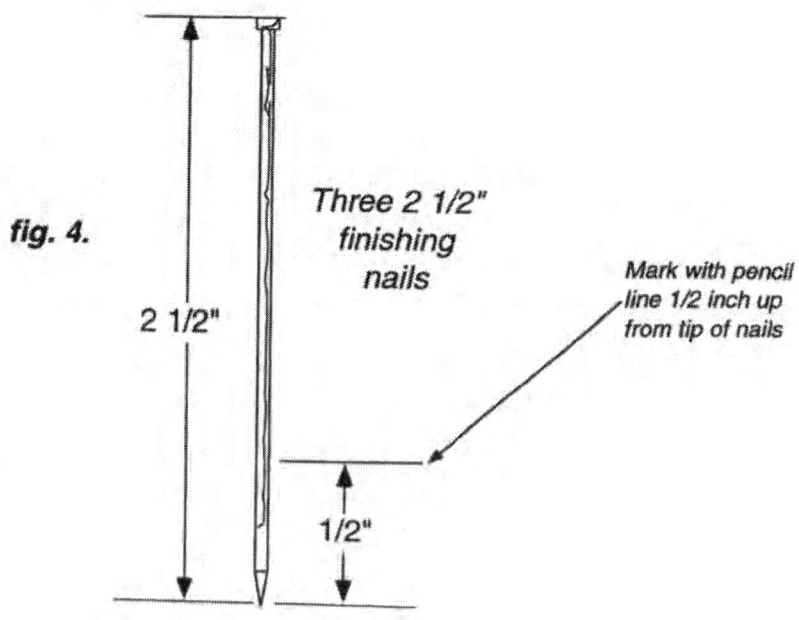

c)
Hammer the three nails into the wood at the locations you created. Stop driving the nail into the wood when it reaches the depth of the pencil line you created (1/2"). Be sure you hammer the nails into the wood as straight as possible.

Wrapping The Wire

a)
Using your wire source create a small loop around any of the nails you hammered into the wood. *fig. 5.* This loop will anchor the wire so it does not slip off the nails while you are wrapping the rest of the wire for the start of the tree. Do not try to hold the wire source in your hand while you are wrapping. Unwrap about 3 feet of wire before you start the wrapping. I find the best way to work with the wire source is to simply let it lay on the floor as you work. Or you can put the wire source into any container that will allow it to move freely so it can unwind the wire as you pull on it. This will make the wrapping process much easier. You may find in the process of wrapping that the wire may sometimes get tangled or twisted. When this happens, stop wrapping and twirl or twist the wire in the opposite direction of the tangle, this will remove the kinks.

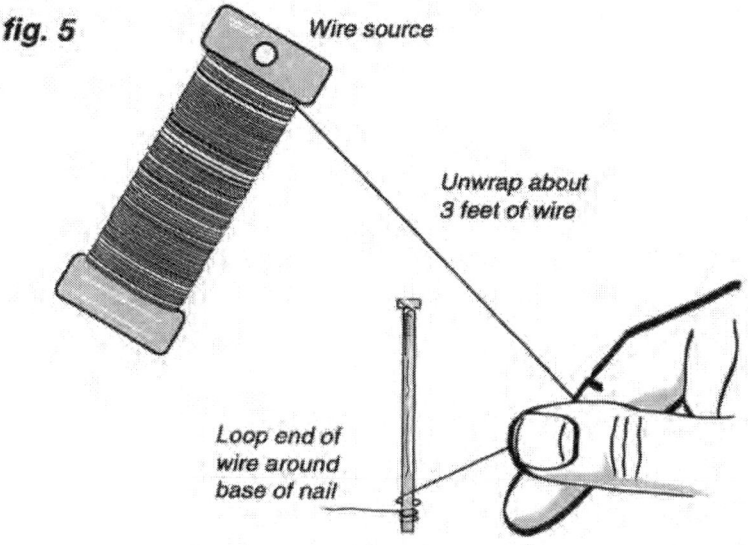

fig. 5
Wire source
Unwrap about 3 feet of wire
Loop end of wire around base of nail

b)
Wrap the wire 35 times around the outside of all three of the finishing nails. *fig. 6.* Do not wrap the wire too tightly. Remember, you will need to slip the wire off the nails when you have finished the wrapping. One wrap is completed when you are back at the point where you started. It does not matter where you start the wrapping or in which direction you proceed. Be sure you keep count of the wraps and end at 35. While you are wrapping, keep the wire bundle as close to the base of the nails as possible, this will prevent the wire from slipping off the tops of the nails as you wrap. If you find that any of the nails are becoming loose while you are wrapping, this is an indication that you are wrapping the wire too tightly around the nails. If this should happen, tap the nails deeper into the wood. If this does not work and the nails have fallen out, you will need to start all over from the beginning.

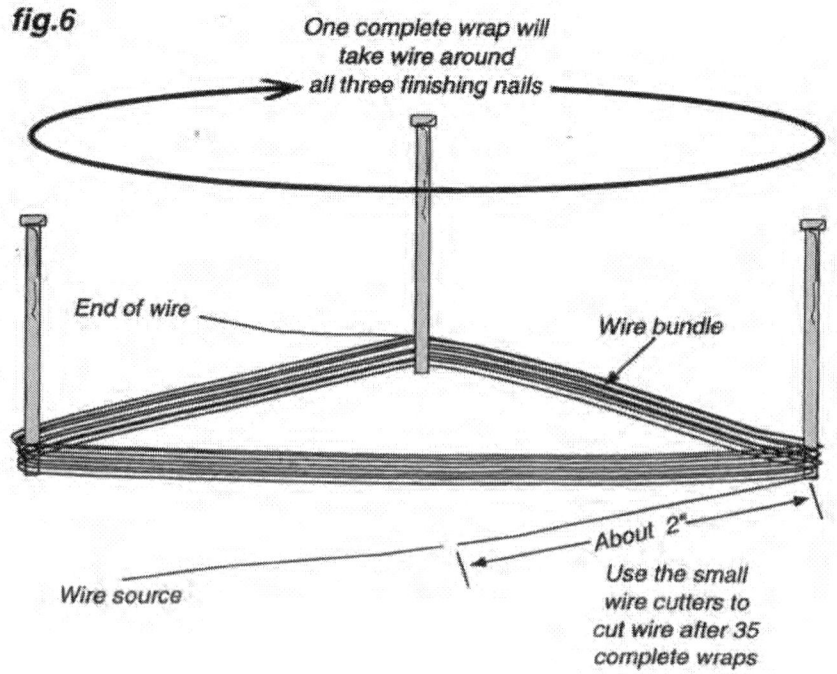

c)
When the wrapping is completed, use the small wire cutters, and carefully cut the wire source about 2" away from the nail where you completed the 35th wrap. Gently slip the wrapped wire bundle off the nails. The wire bundle should look like a triangle with a straight wire at one end and a coiled wire at the other end. Uncoil the small section of wire that was used to hold the wire on the nail when you started. **fig. 7.**

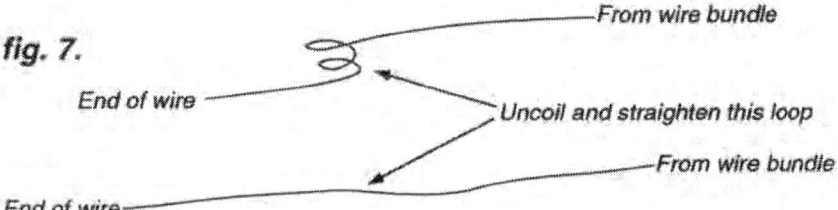

fig. 7.
End of wire
From wire bundle
Uncoil and straighten this loop
From wire bundle
End of wire

NOTE: This completes the need for the jig. You can put it away, however, you may want to use it again to create other tree sculpture. If you want to try to create larger trees you can reposition the finishing nails further apart and add more wraps to the wire bundle. I would suggest that you do not try to create any trees that are over about 6 or 7 inches until you are comfortable with the creation of smaller trees.

d)
Hold the completed bundle of wire in both hands and shape the bundle into an oval. **fig. 8.** Try to unbend, as much as possible, the corners of the wire bundle that were shaped by being wrapped around the nails. Leave both ends of the wire extended out of the bundle. Unwrap one end of the extended wire until it is about 2" long.

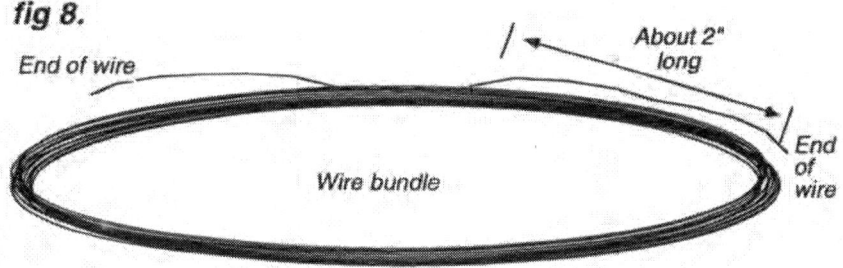

fig 8.
End of wire
About 2" long
Wire bundle
End of wire

e)
Firmly hold the wire bundle about 1/3 the distance in from the curved end of the bundle. **fig. 9.**

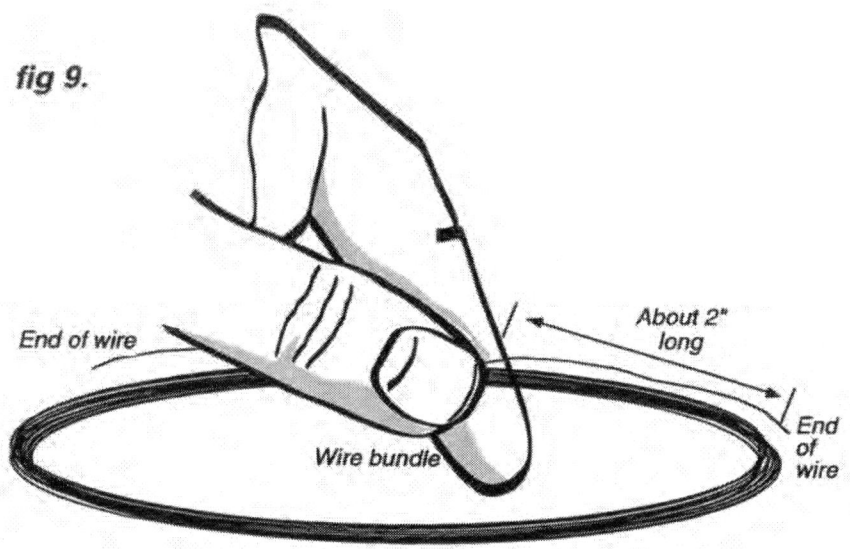

fig 9.

f)
While holding the wire bundle firmly in one hand, use your other hand to bend up the 2" end piece of the wire. **fig. 10.**

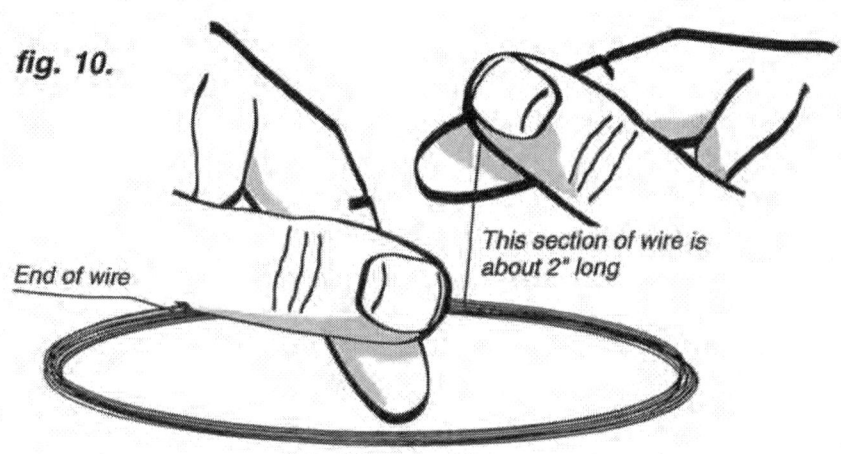

fig. 10.

g)
Wrap the 2" piece of wire around the wire bundle as shown. Keep a firm grip on the wire bundle as you wrap, and wrap the wire as tightly as you can. The first wrappings are important for two reasons. It is this wrap that will hold the bundle together as you work on the tree, and it will also give you a feel for how the wrapping is done. *fig. 11.*

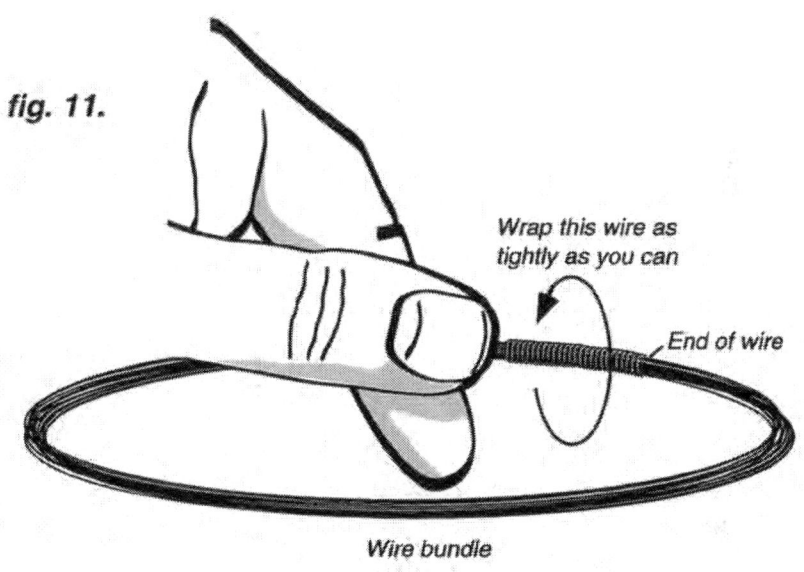

fig. 11.

h)
Using the medium wire cutters, cut through the entire wire bundle about 1" from the curve cloest to the wire coil. It may take a few attempts to cut all the wire, but be sure all the wire is cut. *fig. 12.*

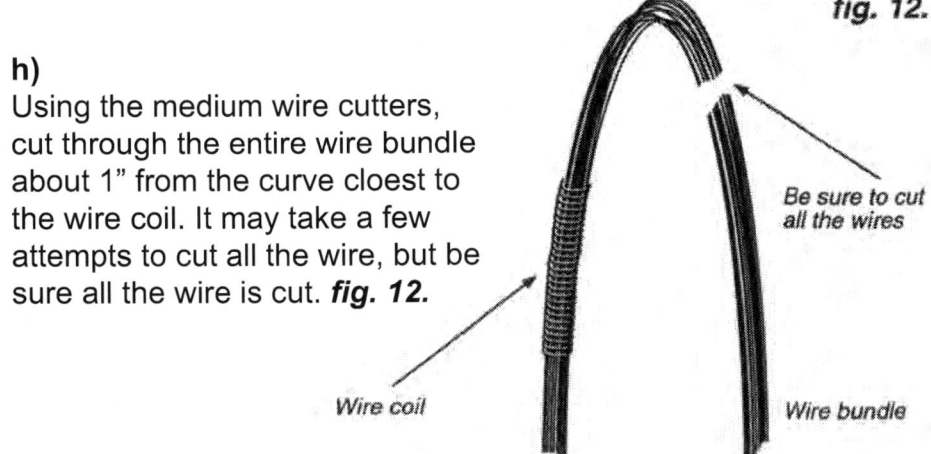

i)
After all the wire in the bundle is cut, unbend both curves in the bundle. *fig. 13.* You should be left with one straight bundle of wire held together by the wire coil near the end of the wire. *fig. 14.*

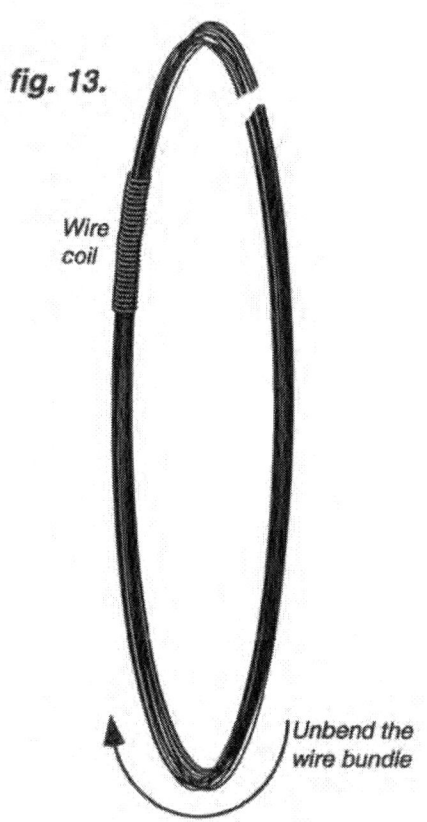

fig. 13.

Wire coil

Unbend the wire bundle

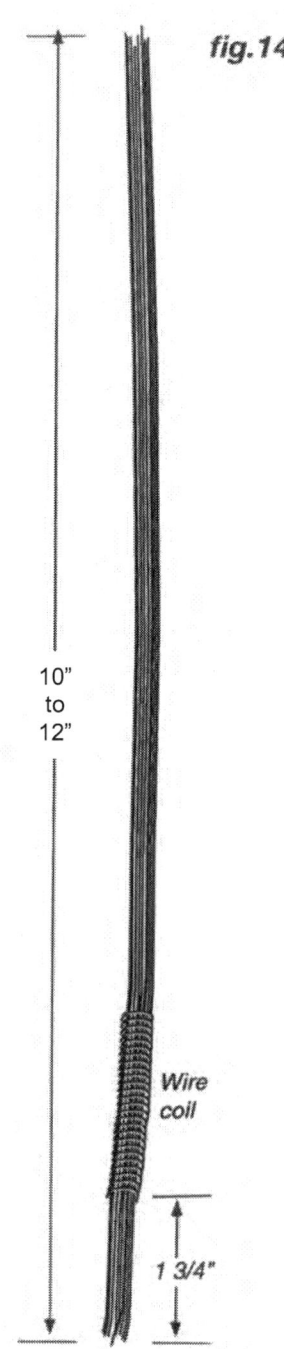

fig.14

10" to 12"

Wire coil

1 3/4"

j)
At this point the wire structure should look like *fig. 14.* The measurements indicated on the illustration do not have to be exactly as stated, however they should be close.

Creating The Root System

I find the root systems of trees very interesting. As with all elements in nature, each tree has a unique character all its own. Some trees have deep roots that show very little detail on the surface, with most of the root system buried deep into the earth. Other trees have roots that appear to be only on the surface of the soil and offering an exciting visual of how they support the structure of the tree. It is the trees that offer this unique view that I find the most interesting.

When you are creating the root system of your tree, do not try to follow exactly what I have illustrated in these pages. Use the techniques shown only as a guide and create a root system that is yours. When creating the root system do not be concerned about counting the wraps or if you are coiling the wire too tight. If the roots you create are a little larger or smaller than I show, it is really not important to the final look of your sculpture. The goal you should strive for is to create a root system that appears to be capable of supporting the tree. When you look at the roots, and they appear to be solid, stable and strong, you have created an effective root system.

The roots I will show you how to create will be partially buried in the "root mound" to help support the tree, therefore it is better to create the roots larger rather than smaller. (I will describe in detail the function and importance of the root mound in the upcoming chapters).

I have found through my years of observing the root systems of trees that in many instances the roots usually grow from the base of the tree in odd numbers at various angles and with many twists and turns.

You are now ready to start wrapping and creating the roots and the rest of the tree. You will be working from the same wire source for the entire tree. This wire will not be cut until the tree sculpture is completely finished.

a)
Holding the wire bundle firmly in the area where the wire coil is, separate the lower part of the root wires into approximately 3 equal sections. *fig. 15.* Do not be concerned if the three sections are not equal. In fact, the root system will look more natural and interesting if the sections are of different sizes and shapes.

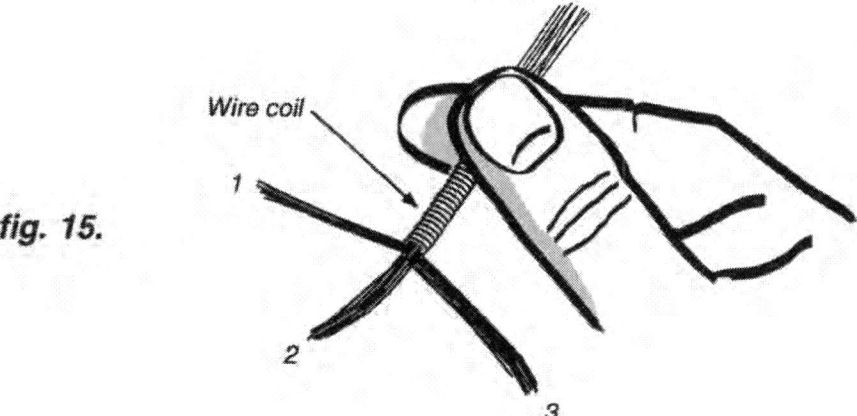

fig. 15.

b)
You are now going to start to wrap the rest of the tree with the wire. Using the source wire, wrap wire tightly up the wire coil toward the top of the tree. *fig. 16.* This first wire wrapping is used to hold all the wire together, so you only need enough to hold the rest of the wire in place as you wrap. This support wire will eventually be wired over when you start to add volume and thickness to the tree trunk.

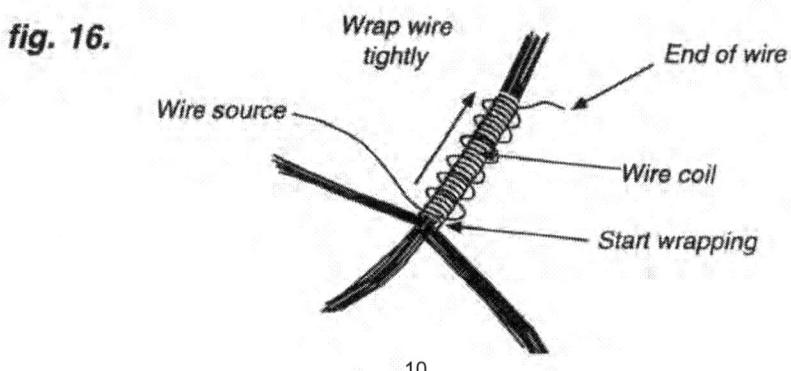

fig. 16.

c)
Using the wire source, start circular wrapping one of the root sections beginning at the base of the trunk and wrapping out toward the end of the root. You can start the wrapping with any of the root sections. Wrap the wire half way down the root section, then stop. At the point where you stopped wrapping the source wire, separate the remaining root sections into 2 or more approximately equal root groups. Loop the wire through the "V" section of the root, then begin wrapping back toward the base of the trunk where you started. *fig. 17.*

d)
Repeat step **c)** for one more of the root sections. The final root section will not be divided into two. This last root section will be created as one large root to add more interest and variation to the entire root system.

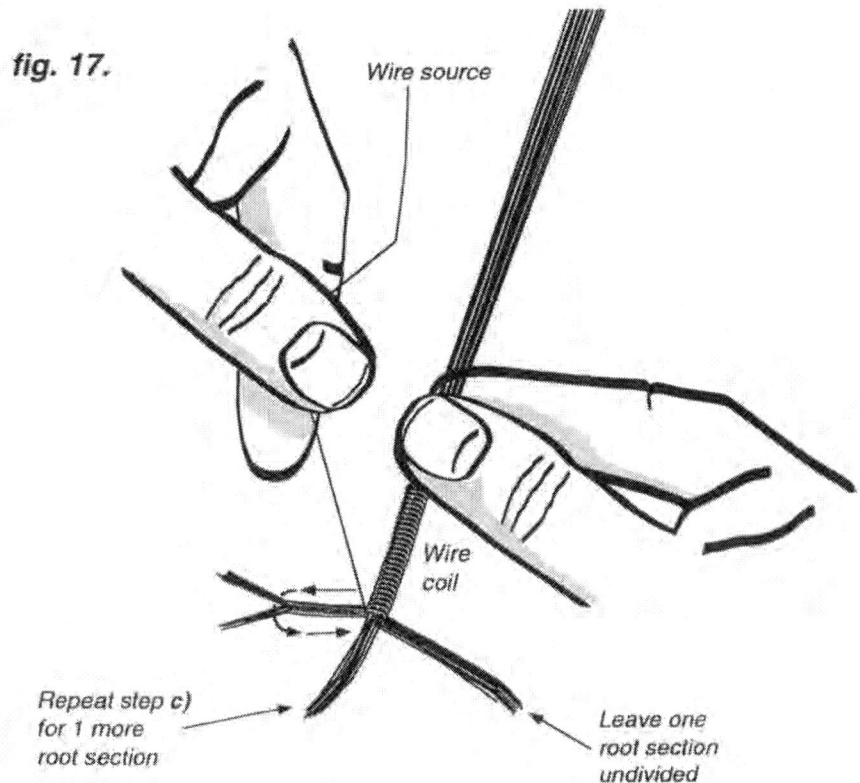

fig. 17.

Wire source

Wire coil

Repeat step c) for 1 more root section

Leave one root section undivided

e)
Separate and fan out all the individual root wires of the final root section. *fig. 18.* This is the section that you did not divide into two parts. This will be the largest of the three root sections. Keep this in mind as you create this section.

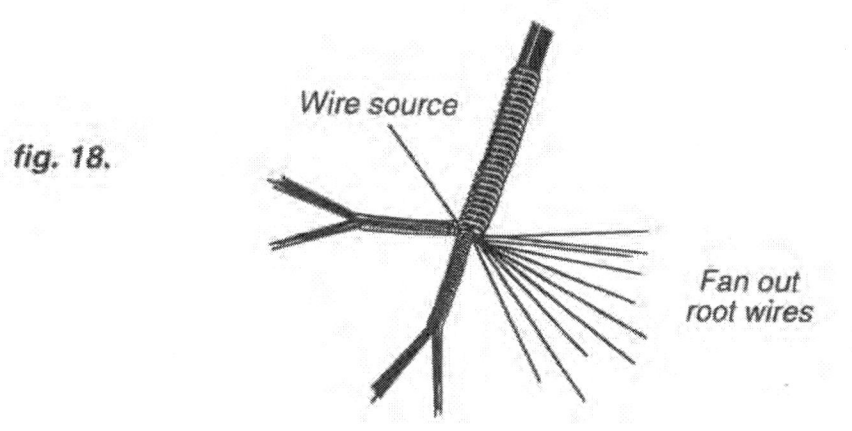

fig. 18.

f)
Starting with the longest of the root wires in this section, using the small wire clippers, snip off the ends of each strand of wire progressively but only slightly smaller than the one before. *fig. 19.* Before you start this step, look carefully at the location where you will be making the cuts. Keep in mind that you can always go back to the wire and clip more off, but you can't go back to add more on!

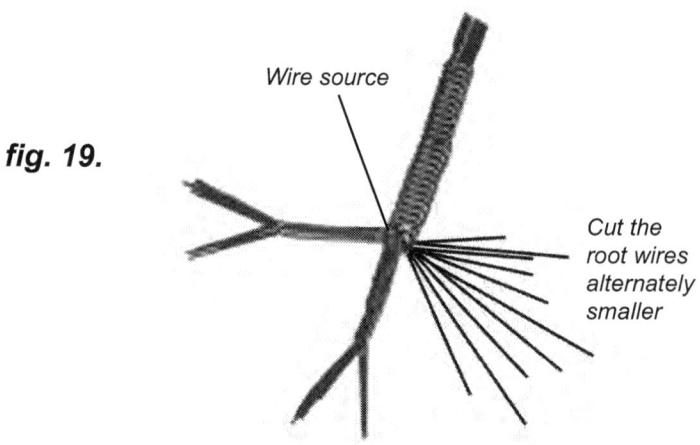

fig. 19.

g)
Repeat the fanning and careful snipping procedure as described in steps **e)** and **f)** for the other smaller root sections.

h)
Working with one root section at a time, squeeze the root wires together to create a total of five root point ends. Since you cut the ends of each root wire to several different lengths, the root section will have a slight taper. This taper will give the root section a much more realistic look. *fig. 20.*

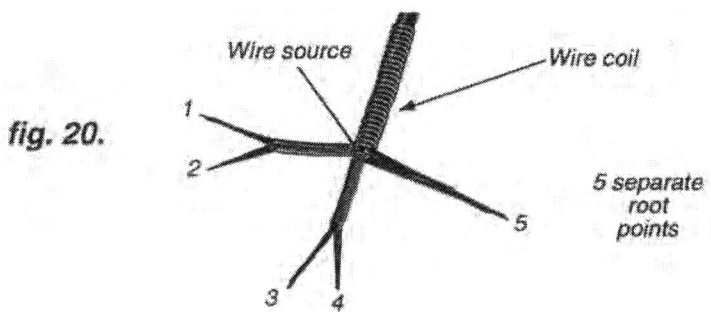
fig. 20.

i)
Using the wire source, slowly and carefully wrap the wire on to each root section. This time, wrap the wire all the way to the end of the root then back to the trunk, then onto the next root section. *fig. 21.* You should end the wrapping of these sections with the wire source at the bottom of the trunk. When you are wrapping the wire around the roots and other parts of the tree, do not try to keep the wire equally spaced or neatly wrapped. Allow the wire to create irregular shapes and little bumps. This technique will create a far more interesting surface texture for the tree.

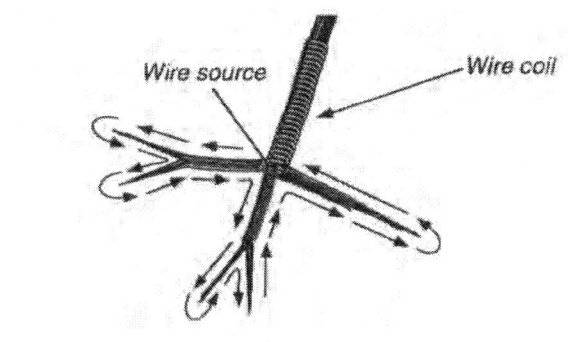
fig. 21.

Wiring The Trunk And The Branches

Wiring the trunk and branches requires the same basic techniques as you used to wire the root system, except now you will need to do much more wiring and over wiring. You should by now be proficient in the process of wiring the tree sculpture. If you feel you are not yet proficient in the process you may want to practice on some scrap wire to create a root system, trunk and branches. Once again, as you are wiring the branches and trunk do not try to keep the wiring equally spaced or smooth. The subtle differences and irregularities in the process of wiring are necessary to give the piece a varied surface texture. You may even want to double back over an area that was previously wired and overwire it for a small section. This doubling back technique will create the little bumps and stubs that are common on so many tree branches and trunks. If you do choose to do some overwiring, only do so for three to five wraps within a small area.

a)
Separate the top section of the tree into two equal parts. (They don't need to be exactly equal). *fig. 22.* Start the separation at the top of the trunk.

b)
Wrap the wire up the trunk to the "V" separation in the branches, then back down the entire trunk to the roots. Repeat this wrapping two or three times, ending the wrapping at the base of the trunk. *fig. 22.*

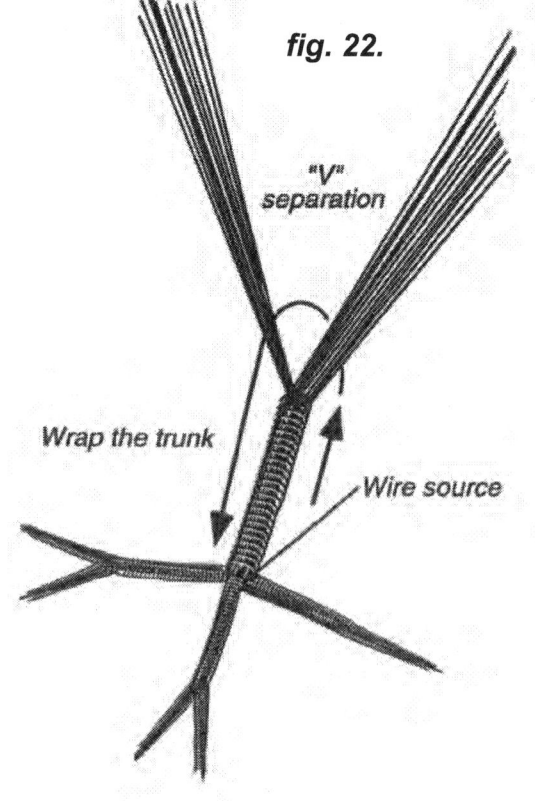

c)
Separate the two main branches into two more equal parts. This will create a total of four branches. ***fig. 23.***

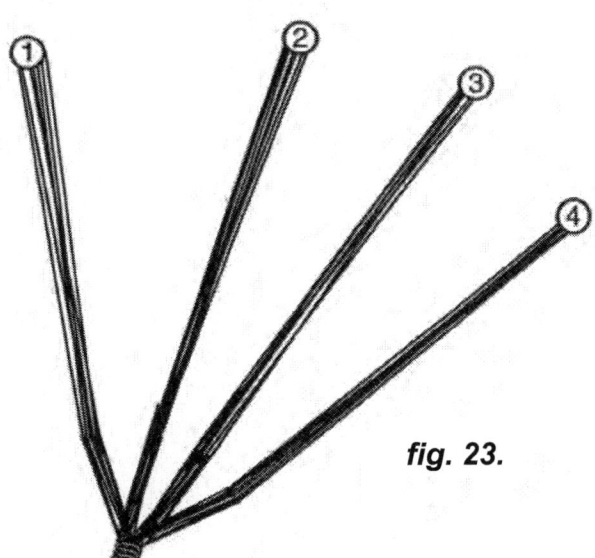

fig. 23.

d)
Wrap the wire up the trunk then onto any one of the four branches you just created. Stop wrapping about one inch up the branch. Separate the wires of this branch into two parts. Pass the wire through the "V" in this branch then continue wiring this branch until you reach the top of the trunk. Repeat this process for all the remaining branches. ***fig. 24.*** After you have finished all the wiring you will have created a total of eight branches.

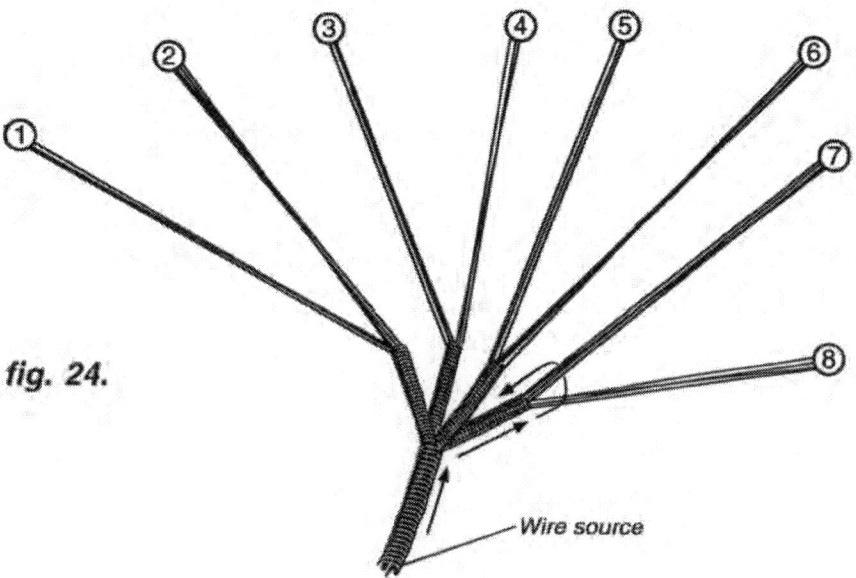

fig. 24.

Forming The Tree

a) - *See fig. 26 for a), b), c) & d) steps on this page.*
Spread out the three root sections of the tree to form a tripod. Though the tree sculpture is not yet complete and may be thin, it should be able to stand on the root base you created.

b)
Twist two of the branches together at their base to form one larger branch with the two smaller branches "growing" out of the larger one.

c)
Gently bend the top section of the three root sections in toward the trunk to create a section that looks like a step.

d)
Gently bend all three roots at varied irregular angles. None of the roots should be straight. At this point you should also create a slight bend in the trunk.

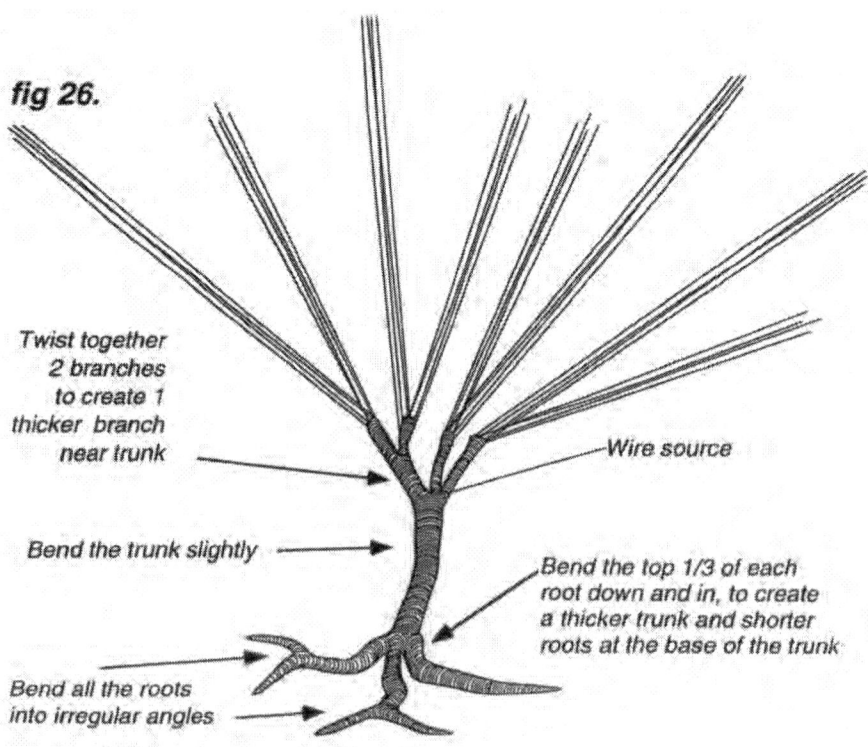

fig 26.

Twist together 2 branches to create 1 thicker branch near trunk

Wire source

Bend the trunk slightly

Bend the top 1/3 of each root down and in, to create a thicker trunk and shorter roots at the base of the trunk

Bend all the roots into irregular angles

e)
Wrap the wire down the trunk and onto each of the root sections. Do not wrap the wire to the tip of each root, but stop the wrapping and return to the trunk when you are about half way to the tip of the root. Wrap all the tops of the root sections that are closest to the trunk. This will create a trunk base that is the thickest part of the tree and it will look very realistic. End the wrapping at the top of the trunk. *fig. 27.*

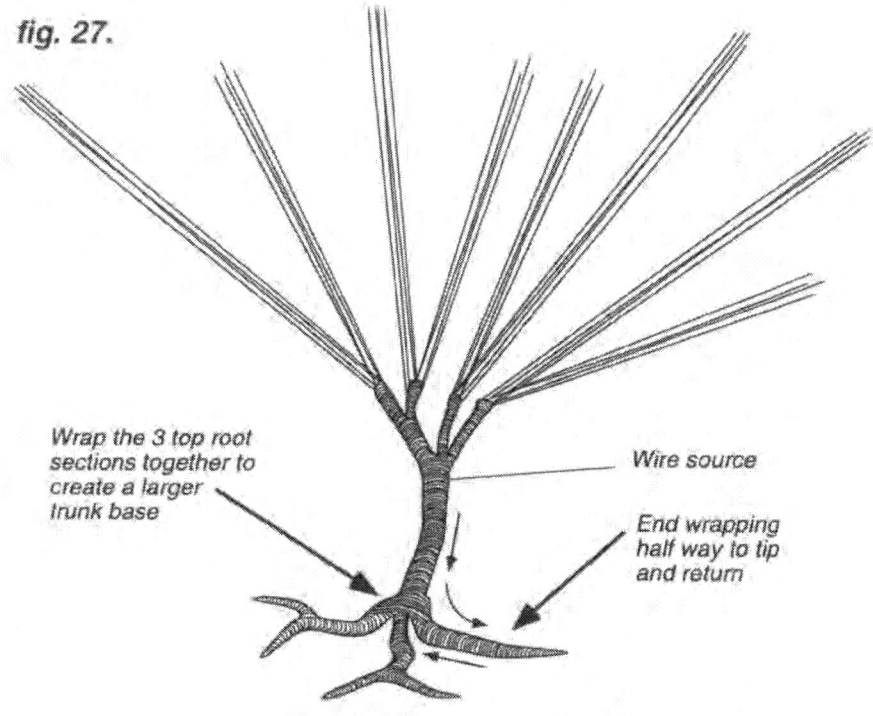

fig. 27.

Wrap the 3 top root sections together to create a larger trunk base

Wire source

End wrapping half way to tip and return

Thickening The Tree

a)
Continue wrapping the tree to thicken the trunk and roots. Do not wrap the wire all the way to the tip of the roots, but stop and return to different points along the way. *fig. 27.*

b)
Wrap the base of the trunk and the area where the roots enter the trunk several more times so they are thicker in these areas. You should continue to wrap the tree until you feel it is thick enough and looks good to you. Once the tree is fully wrapped, if you should feel it needs more thickness, you can always go back and add more wire. *fig. 28.*

c)
Apply the same procedure for the branches as you did for the roots. However, this time wire all the way to the end of the thicker branch coil, then return. Repeat this wrapping process for all the branches. *fig. 28.*

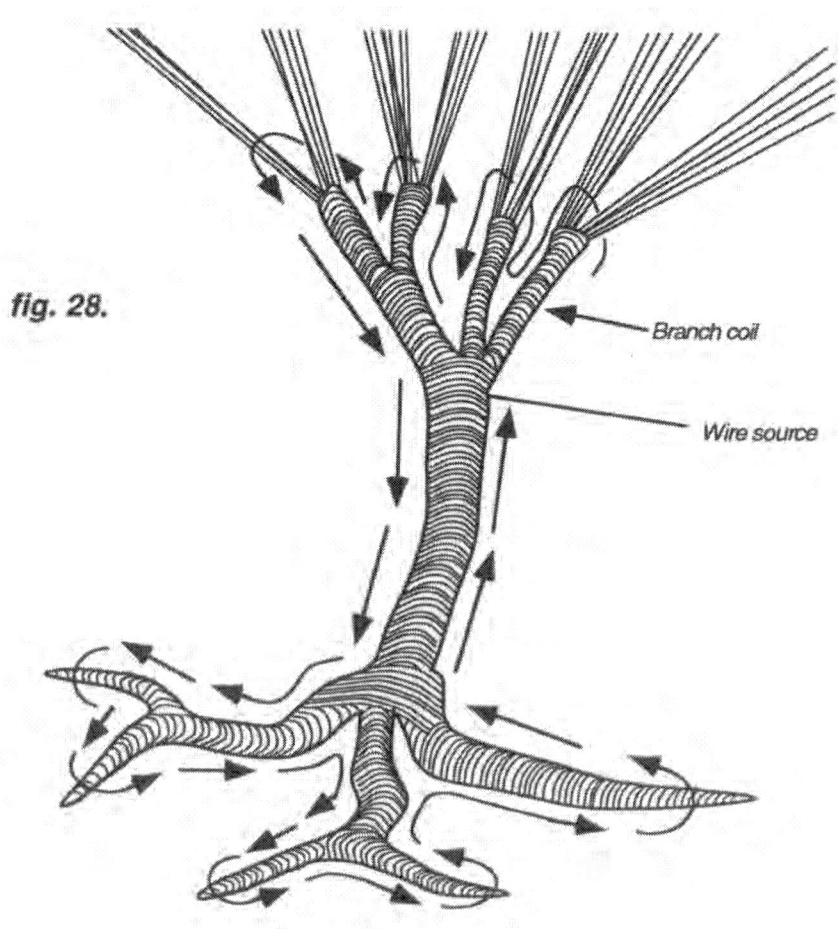

fig. 28.

Branch coil

Wire source

The Final Branching

a) *Use fig. 29 for steps a), b), & c).*
Separate the remaining wire of each branch into two approximately equal amounts. You will find that some of the remaining branches will have even amounts and some will have odd amounts. This is not a problem and will be addressed in later steps.

b)
Twist, as tightly as you can, each separate group of wire together to create an entirely new thicker branch. Twist the wire until the new branch you are creating is about one inch long. After you complete this step, you should have about sixteen branches in your tree.

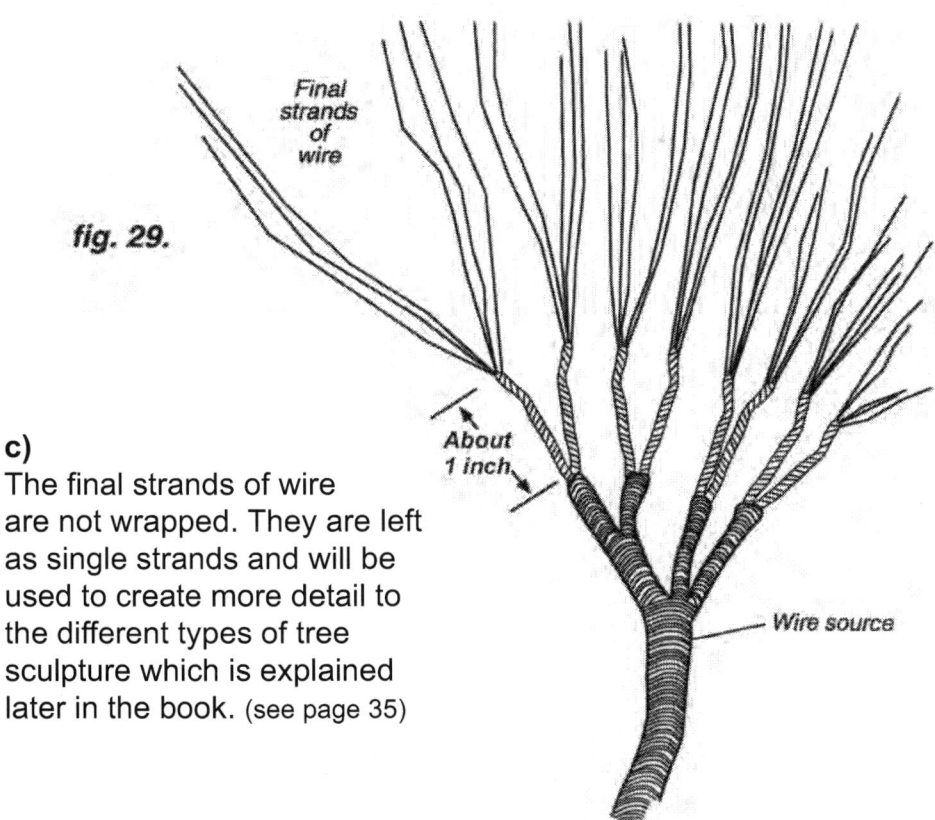

fig. 29.

c)
The final strands of wire are not wrapped. They are left as single strands and will be used to create more detail to the different types of tree sculpture which is explained later in the book. (see page 35)

Creating The Root Anchors

The final use of the wire source is to create an anchor that will hold the tree onto the base material. This anchor will not be seen when the tree sculpture is completed.

a)
Wrap the wire down the trunk and half way onto any root. Keep in mind that this wrap will be seen, so try to keep it consistent with the look of the trunk. Do not try to wrap too quickly to get to the base. *fig. 30.*

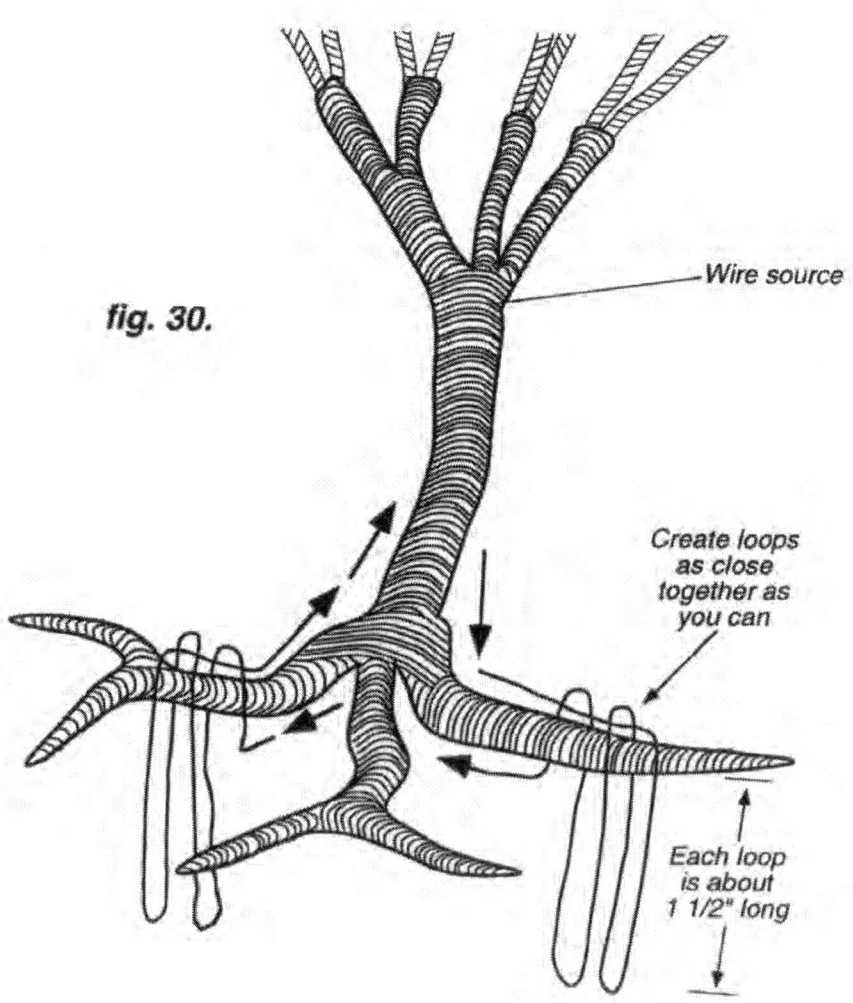

fig. 30.

b)
Twist the double loops together to create one thick loop. Repeat this process for the other root anchor wires. Be sure to twist the wires as tightly as you can so it is wrapped close to the bottom of the root. *fig. 31.*

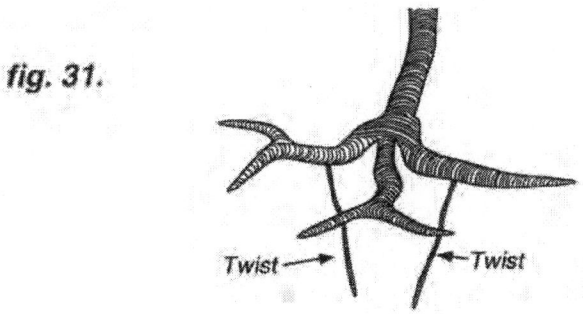

fig. 31.

c)
Twist both double anchor wires together about half way up their distances. This will create one large root anchor that will be bonded into the root mound. This root anchor will not be visible when the tree is completed. *fig. 32.*

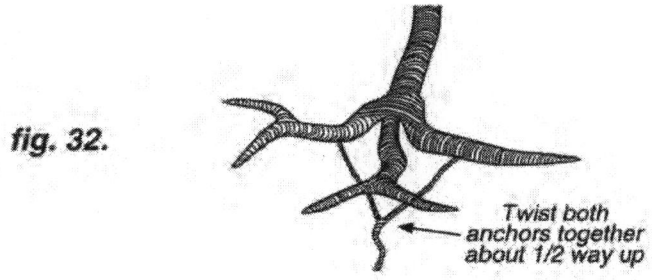

fig. 32.

At this stage your creation, with all its twists, bends, bumps and curves, should actually start to look like a tree. *fig. 33.* As you look at your tree, If you feel the trunk, branches, or roots are too thin or not in the correct proportion, it is not too late to go back and add thickness or form to where you think it is needed. Simply get the end of the wire source, twist a small piece onto the main root anchor and if you want to work on the roots or trunk, wrap as needed. To add onto the branches, once again twist a small piece onto one of the twigs, and wrap as needed.

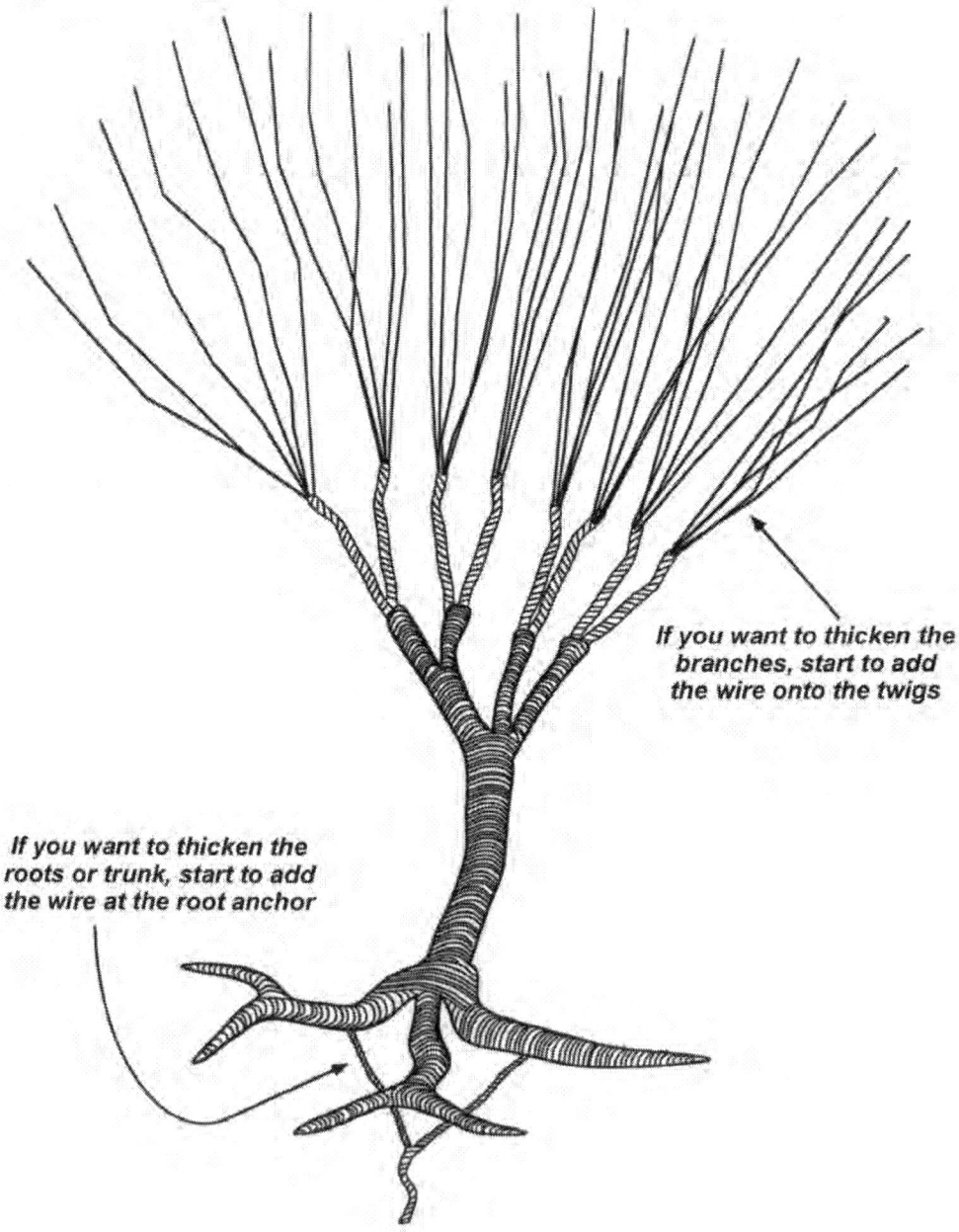

fig. 33.

If you want to thicken the branches, start to add the wire onto the twigs

If you want to thicken the roots or trunk, start to add the wire at the root anchor

Preparing The Tree For Mounting

a)
Hold the tree firmly by the trunk and gather all of the branches together then point them up. This will help to keep the branches out of the way as you proceed. *fig. 34.*

b)
Still holding the tree firmly, gather the roots together and point them down. Tuck the anchor wires into the center of the roots. The tree is now ready to be mounted onto the base. Place it aside as we prepare the base for the root mound.

NOTE: At this point your tree is ready for shaping and mounting. Your selection of the style of tree you want will be made after the tree is mounted onto the base.
(see page 35)

fig. 34.

Point all the branches upward

Tuck all the anchor wire under and within the roots

Point all the roots downard

Point all the roots downard

Preparing The Base For The Tree

You can use any porous material as a base on which to mount your tree, such as rocks, pottery, wood, glass, etc.. Just be sure the base you select is compatible with the white glue you will be using to bond the roots to the base. Before starting, read the label on the glue package and it will list the type of surfaces the glue will bond with. The shape and style of the tree has not yet been selected. You will do this when the tree is permanently mounted onto the base. When selecting the size and shape of the base, be sure it does not visually overpower the size of the tree. The mass of the base should be optically only a little bit larger than the tree. After you have created the tree and mounted it on the base, should you find you are not pleased with the mounting, you can separate the tree and the base by placing them in clean warm water for a few hours. Since the white glue is water soluble it will dissolve and release the roots. After the tree dries, you can try again. For the tree shown I have selected a piece of free formed dark glass that I purchased in an art and crafts store.

a)
Place a piece of double stick tape or fold over a piece of masking tape onto the bottom of the base. Use enough tape to hold the base securely. This tape will hold the base in position in the tray you will be using as you work on creating the root mound. *fig. 35*

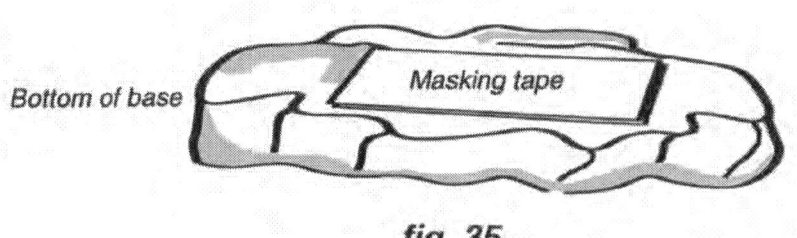

fig. 35.

b)
Place the base, tape side down, in the center of the tray or source you are using to work in. Press the base firmly onto the tray to be sure the tape is holding fast. *fig. 36.* The base and the tree sculpture will stay in this tray for the entire process of creating the root mound.

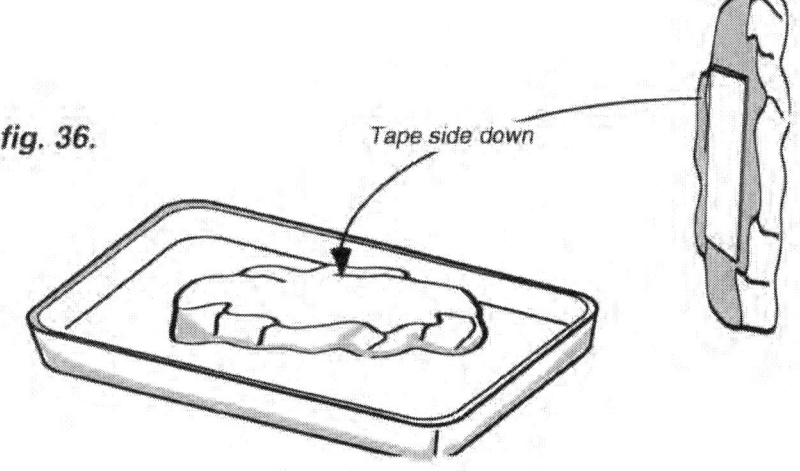

fig. 36.

Tape side down

c)
Put four or five drops of the white glue onto the center of the base. Be careful not to get any glue on the tray (you don't want to glue the base to the tray). If you do find the glue is running over the sides and onto the tray, wipe the base and the tray clean and start over again. This glue spot will be the start of the root mound. *fig. 37.*

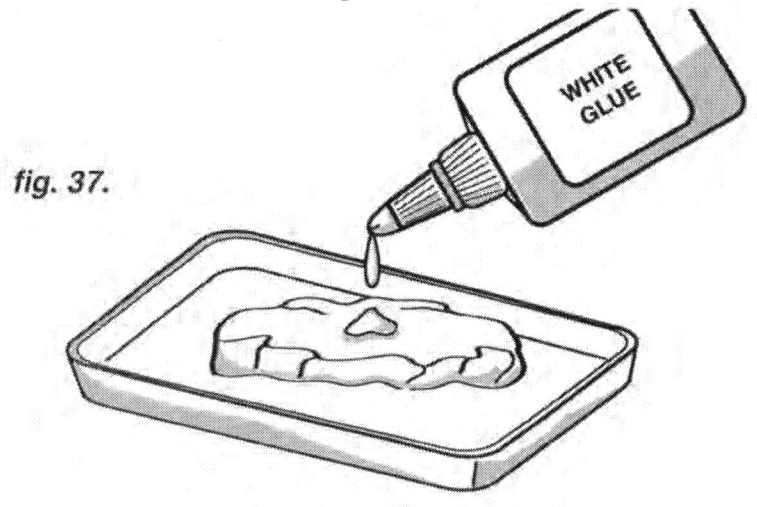

fig. 37.

d)
Sprinkle on enough sand to cover the entire glue spot. I like to use an old spoon, but you can just sprinkle it on by hand if you like. Don't be concerned about putting on too much sand. The glue spot will only absorb as much as it can hold, and the rest of the sand will remain loose. Let this mixture dry overnight. *fig. 38.* From this point on, the glue mixture will be called the root mound.

fig. 38.

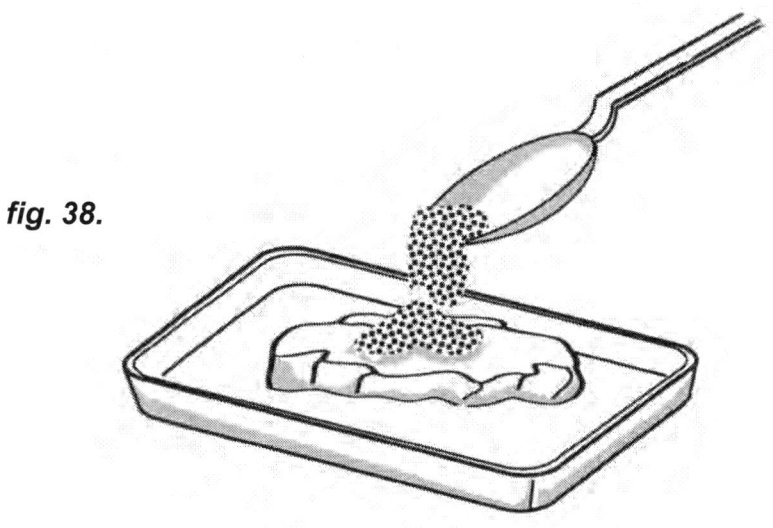

e)
After you are sure the glue is dry, use the soft brush to remove the excess sand from the top of your base. Simply brush the sand into the tray. *fig. 39.*

fig. 39.

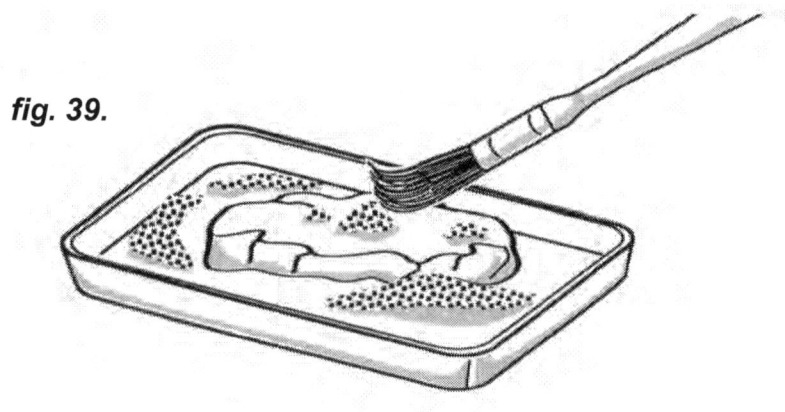

Mounting The Tree Onto The Base

The tree will be bound onto the base in several steps. The first few steps will bond the tree to the mound and the remaining steps will create an interesting support structure from which the roots will appear to be growing. Once again, each time you apply a layer of the glue and sand mixture it should be throughly dried before the next layer is applied.

a)
Spread the three root sections slightly apart. At about the half way point of each root section bend the root upward so it will support the tree. Gently but firmly push the tree down on the base so that the three main root sections begin to spread out. Be sure the anchor wire is tucked within and under the root area. Try to spread the root sections equally. The root sections should be optically spaced. *fig. 40.*

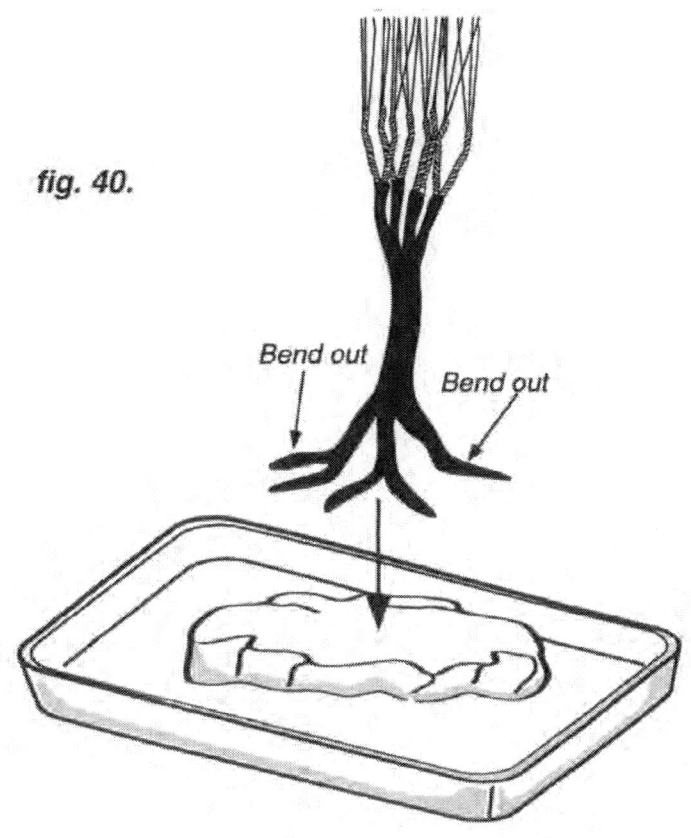

fig. 40.

b)
After the roots are spread out, the tree will be able to stand erect on the base. Using the masking tape, tape the tree to the tray. Apply tape only to the bottom of the tree, over the root section. *fig. 41.* This taping step is only a temporary hold until we secure the entire tree to the tray.

fig. 41.

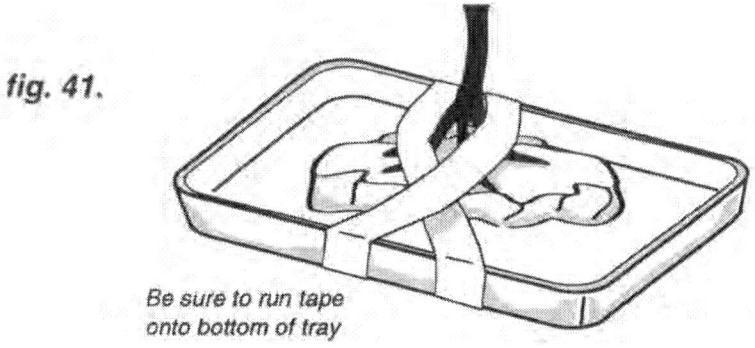

Be sure to run tape onto bottom of tray

c)
Gently hold the tree by the trunk and divide the branches into two approximately equal groups. Fold the branches over and tape them to the sides and bottom of the tray. This will hold the tree securely in place for the rest of the gluing procedure. Be sure the branches are securely fastened to the tray, Use plenty of tape! *fig. 42.*

d)
When you are sure the tree is securely fastened to the tray by the branches you can carefully remove the tape that is on the root section.

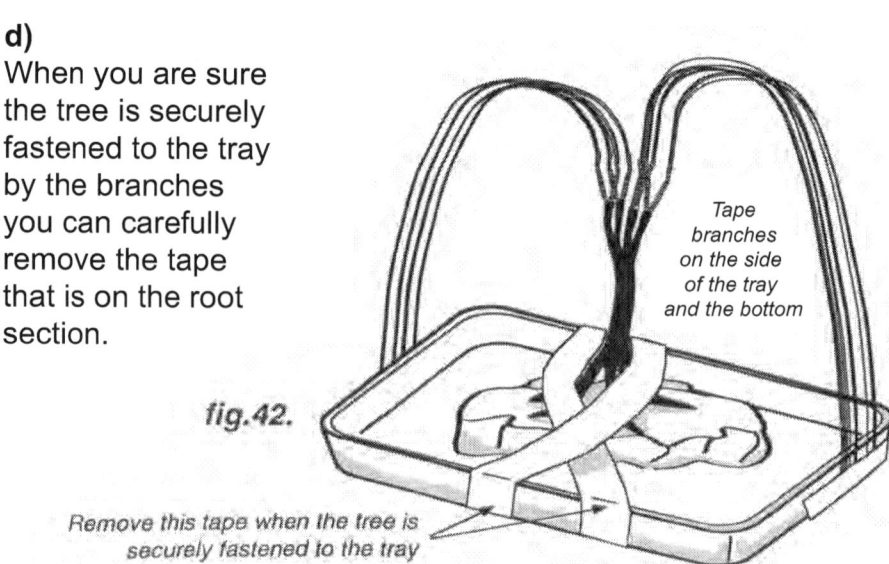

Tape branches on the side of the tray and the bottom

fig.42.

Remove this tape when the tree is securely fastened to the tray

Creating The Root Mound

The root mound is very important to the overall appearance of the tree sculpture. The structural purpose of the root mound is of course, to hold the tree onto the base. The visual purpose of it is to create the appearance that the tree is growing out of the center of the mound. To these ends, it is much better to have less root mound rather than more. All the roots of the tree will look much more realistic if they are only slightly imbedded in the mound, not covered by it. The top third of each root section, as a minimum, should be visible. To ensure the strength of the structure it is very important that each application of the sand and glue mixture is completely dry and solid before you stare the next step. If you want to speed up the drying you can place the piece under a lamp with a regular 60 watt bulb in it. Place the piece as close to the bulb as you can. However do not allow the bulb to actually touch or rest on the tree sculpture. This will cut the drying time in half.

a) Construct a "sand dam" around the entire base of the trees root system. The tips of the roots should be entirely buried in the sand, but the center of the tree, directly under the trunk must not have any sand on it. This void will be filled with the sand and glue mixture and will be the start of binding the tree to the base. After you create the sand dam you should be able to see the original small glue and sand mound you first created. *fig. 43.* If you find you have used too much sand to create the sand dam, carefully dump out all the sand and start again.

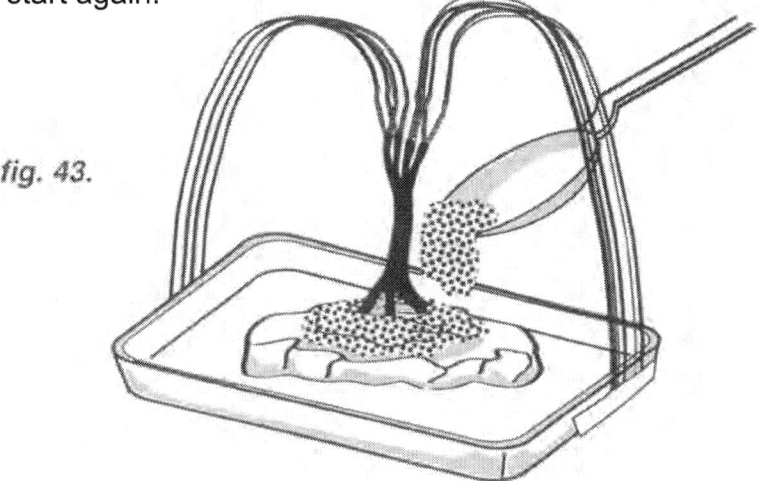

fig. 43.

b)
Apply about 15 to 20 drops of the white glue directly into the center of the sand dam. *fig. 44.* Be very careful not to apply too much glue. You can always add more, but it is very dificult to remove the glue. The total amount of glue should fill the void in the center only about half way. The sand dam will hold the glue in place as you proceed to the next step. This is where most people run into dificultly. Proceed slowly during these steps. It is much better to apply too little glue than too much. Keep in mind that the root mound will be created in layers not as one huge mound!

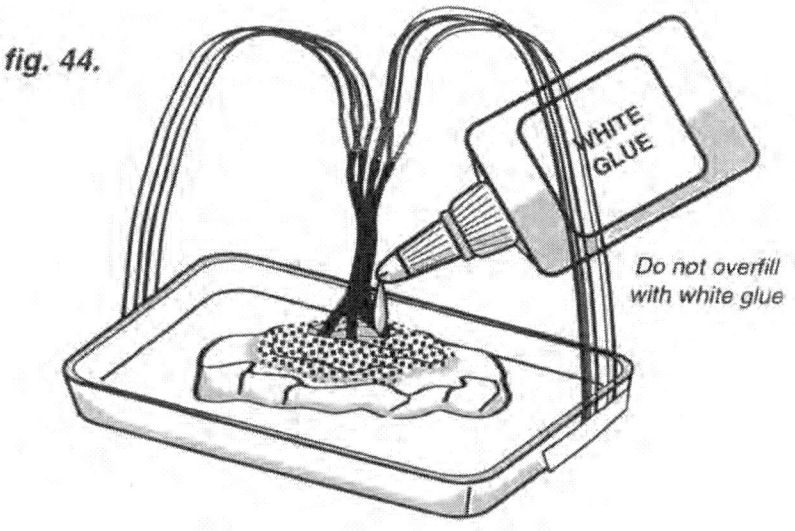

fig. 44.

Do not overfill with white glue

c)
Slowly add additional sand to the rim of the sand dam until the entire center of the root area is covered. Get the sand from your source, not from the sand you created the root mound with. Add the sand from the outer edge toward the center of the tree as you proceed around. As you are adding the sand you will see that it is being absorbed with the glue. Add the sand slowly and carefully and only a very little at a time. Do not move the tree as you are adding the sand. When you are finished adding the sand, you should not be able to see any of the root structure. *fig. 45.*

d)
After you are sure the sand mound is completely dry, brush away all the loose sand from around the roots and inside the root area. Save all this sand, you can use it again. Since the tree is now securely fastened to the root mound and to the tray you can dump out any excess sand as you hold the tree, base and tray.

e)
Build another sand dam as you did before. This time construct the dam so that when you fill it with the glue and sand mixture it will reach to the bottom of the trunk area. Again, if you find you have too much sand for the dam, dump it out and start again.

f)
For this layer add about 10 to 15 drops of glue onto the center of the root mound and cover the entire sand dam with sand. Let it dry completely.

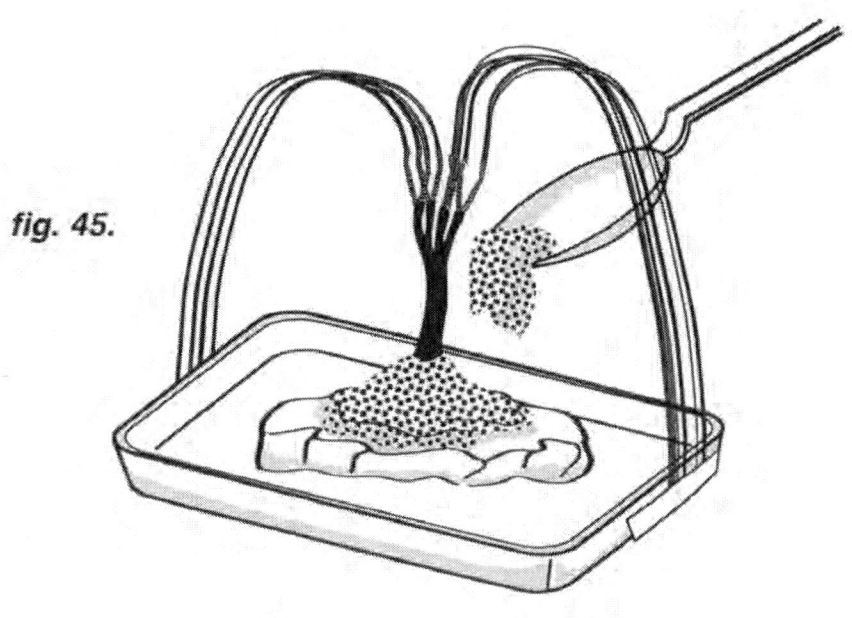

fig. 45.

Final Construction Of The Root Mound

a)
When you are sure the sand dam is completely dry and hard to the touch, brush away all the loose sand then dump any excess sand out of the tray.

b)
If you see any voids or spaces in the root mound that you would like to fill in, add 1 or 2 drops of glue in the void, then add the sand and cover the entire area as you did before. If any of the voids are large enough to require more than a few drops of glue, fill these in one layer at a time. As an alternative to filling the larger voids with just sand, you can also place small pebbles or sea shells in the void and glue them in place using the glue and sand. When ever you add glue to the sand mound for any reason you must also add sand. This will prevent any area of the root mound to show only the dried glue, which does not look very nice. I find the root systems look more interesting and realistic if they have less sand and glue mixture, rather than more. The root mound should look like it can easily support the entire tree but it should not over power it or hide too much of the roots.

c)
After you are satisfied with the way the roots and the root mound look, you can carefully remove all the tape and take the tree sculpture off the tray. If you should find any areas on the root mound that are not dry and have some wet glue on them, simply sprinkle more sand over that area and let it dry.

d)
You are now ready to decide whether you want to leave the root mound as a natural sand mound, or if you would prefer to have the sand look like moss covered earth. If you wish to keep the root mound natural, with no color, skip the next step, *"Adding color to the root mound".*

Adding Color To The Root Mound

a)
To add color to the mound that will look like moss covered earth, you will need yellow, green and white India ink. Any brand of colored in will due. Just be sure it is ink, not paint! Through trail and error I have found that ink is the best medium to use on the root mound. The ink will soak into the sand and it will keep its bright color for years. The ink is also very opaque and the colors will not run into each other as long as you follow my technique for applying the ink. This ink will not come out in the wash, so don't get it on your clothing. Please do not use water colors acrylics or oil paint for the root mound. I have tried them all and they just don't work for this application. You can buy the colored ink in any store that sells art and crafts supplies, and of course you can get it from the internet. You will use very little ink for each tree, so buy the smallest amount you can. You will also need a small, soft inexpensive artists or crafters brush. Size "1" will do fine. After you have finished using your brush wash it off with warm water and a bit of soap, rinse in clean water and let it dry thoroughly before you go on to the next color. If you let the brush sit with the ink in the bristles the brush will dry rock hard.

b)
Before you start the coloring of the root mound, carefully bend all of the branches straight up. This will keep all the wire out of your way as you work.

c)
Starting with the green ink and the small brush, apply the color onto the root mound. You will notice that the sand of the mound will actually draw the ink out of the brush and into the sand. Do not attempt to "paint" the sand. Let the ink be absorbed into the sand. Color only about 3/4 of the overall area of the mound with green. And also keep in mind that you will be leaving about 10% of the mound with no color on it at all. This effect will give the root mound a very natural appearance. Try not to get any of the ink on any part of the actual tree, if you do, wipe it off as soon as you can.

If the sand you are using is a mixture of items like small pebbles, shells, pieces of wood or glass, try to leave these items uncolored and natural. This subtle contrast in color and texture will add to the realism of the piece and give it much more depth. Proceed slowly, once the ink is on it is very difficult to remove. If you should get any color on the tree itself, you will need to scrape it off with a razor blade or some other sharp tool. It is much better not to get any on any of the tree or the base. Again, as soon as you finish using the brush wash it off with warm water and a bit of soap, rinse in clean water and let it dry thoroughly before you go on to the next color.

d)
After the green color is dry, and your brush is dry, usually about 3 hours, apply the yellow color. Use the same absorption technique as you did for the green color. Apply only about 1/4 the amount of yellow as you did green. This will make the green the dominate color on the root mound. Try not to get any of the yellow on any of the natural forms or on the tree.

e)
After the yellow and your brush is dry you will be applying the final color, white. The white is used only as a highlight so you need only apply a small amount to get the desired effect. Apply the white using only the tip of the brush. Use only enough white to cover only about 10% of the area. You will be amazed how bright and white this ink is and how little you need to create the desired effect. When you finish adding the white let the piece dry. If you feel you need to add more of any color you can still do so. Since these colors are opaque you will be able to add any color over an other color. It is a good idea to add any additional color in the same order as you did in the beginning; green, yellow, white. When you have finished adding all the colors and have let all dry, you are finished with the root mound. Do not add or apply any other coating or protective spray to the root mound, you will just be dulling the colors. If, in a few years you see the colors have dulled due to dust or dirt, you can clean the piece with a damp cloth and apply fresh ink colors.

Creating The Style Of Tree Sculpture You Want

Your tree sculpture is now ready for the final steps. Using the basic tree shape you just created you can form and change the trunk, branches and twigs into any of the following 5 different tree styles:

Weeping Willow, Beaded, Wind Swept, Oak and Bonsai with Leaves.

Weeping Willow. (page 36) This is by far the easiest of all the trees to form and requires very little, if any, additional cutting and shaping.

Beaded. (page 41) This very decorative tree is created by adding glass fringe beads to the basic Weeping Willow tree.

Wind Swept. (page 45) To create the Wind Swept you will need to re-shape the trunk and trim some of the branches and twigs.

Oak Tree. (page 50) The Oak tree is the most difficult to create. Its creation requires bending, twisting, re-shaping and cutting of the branches and twigs. After you have created an Oak tree you will be able to create larger and more difficult tree sculptures.

Bonsai with Leaves. (page 60) Similar to creating the Oak tree, but the ends of the twigs are hammered flat to look like leaves.

NOTE: If this is your first attempt at creating wire tree sculpture, I would suggest that you start with the Weeping Willow.

Creating The Weeping Willow

Of all the tree sculpture described in this book, the weeping willow is by far the easiest to create. This tree requires very little, if any, cutting and shaping and creating it will give you a feel for working with the wire before you move on to more difficult creations.

a)
Hold the tree firmly by the trunk. This is the best way to hold the tree securely as you work on it. This grip will allow you to turn and view it from different angles to be sure you are creating the shape you want.

b)
Spread out all the branches so they look like a fan. All the branches should be flat on the same plane. At this point the tree will look flat, we will create the roundness and fullness later on. *fig. 46.*

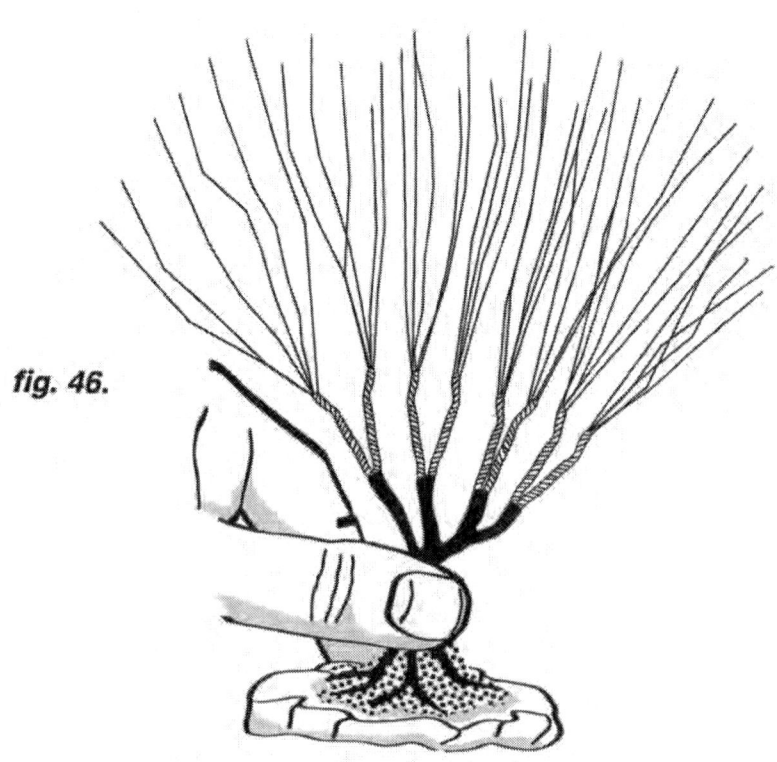

fig. 46.

c)
Hold the tree firmly at the top section of the trunk with one hand. With your other hand grip any two outermost branches at the "V" section. Now twist the branches toward you half a turn. *fig. 47.* This action will result in the two branches you have twisted becoming perpendicular to the branches next to them. The tree will now start to have a more rounded and full appearance.

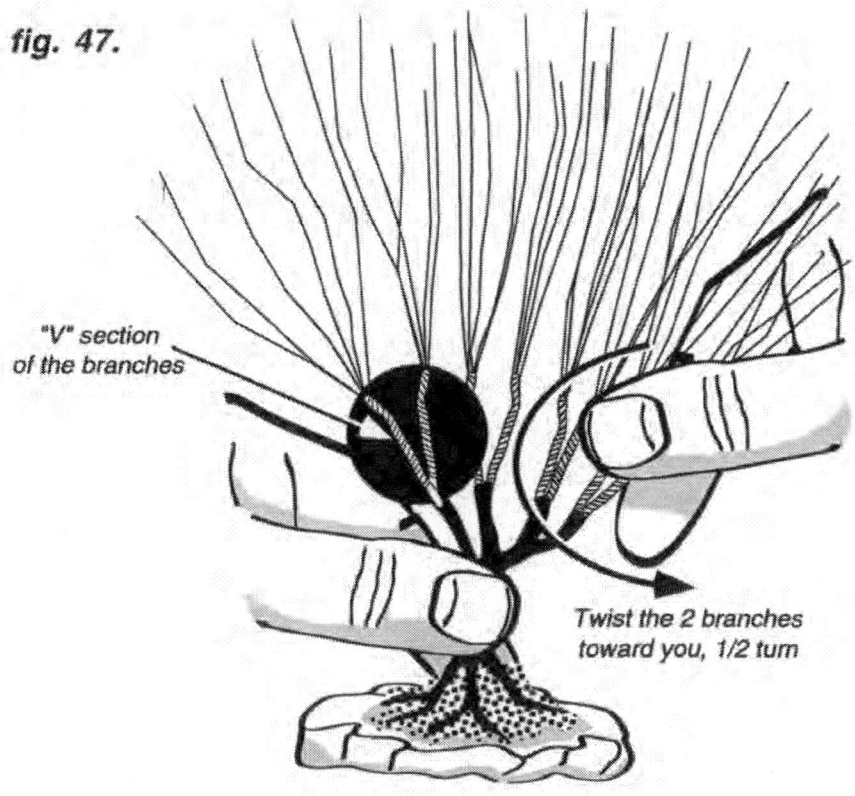

fig. 47.

"V" section of the branches

Twist the 2 branches toward you, 1/2 turn

d)
Holding the tree at the point where the branches start to extend out of the trunk, place your index finger about half way up the branch. Start bending the twig wires over the top roundness of your index finger until all the twig end of the branches point directly down. As you are bending the the wires, try not to bend all the wire at the same point. Move your finger to a place on the next branch that was different than the previous one. This will help with creating a more realistic group of branches and twigs. For more of a variety in the bending of the branches and twigs, bend the wires one at a time. *fig. 48.* After bending all the wires, if you are not happy with the look of the tree, you can very easily un-bend all or part of the wire and start again.

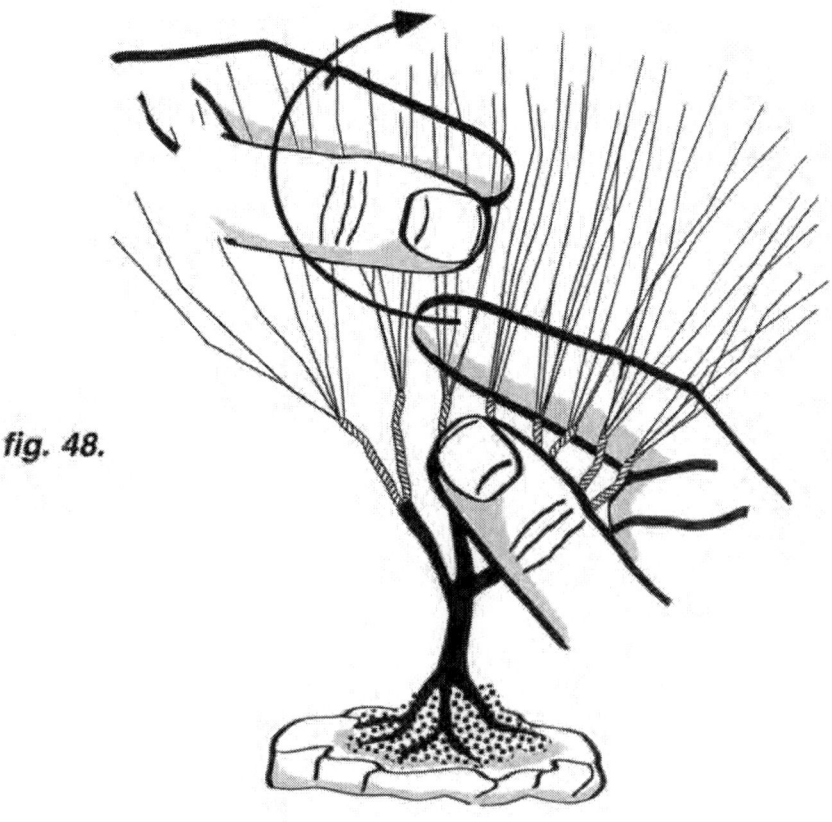

fig. 48.

e)
As you are bending the branches, stop for a moment to look at the tree from above looking directly down at it. ***fig. 49.*** The tree when viewed from this vantage point, should have a round or oval shape. If you think your tree looks flat, pull the branches away from each other to create the desired round or oval effect.

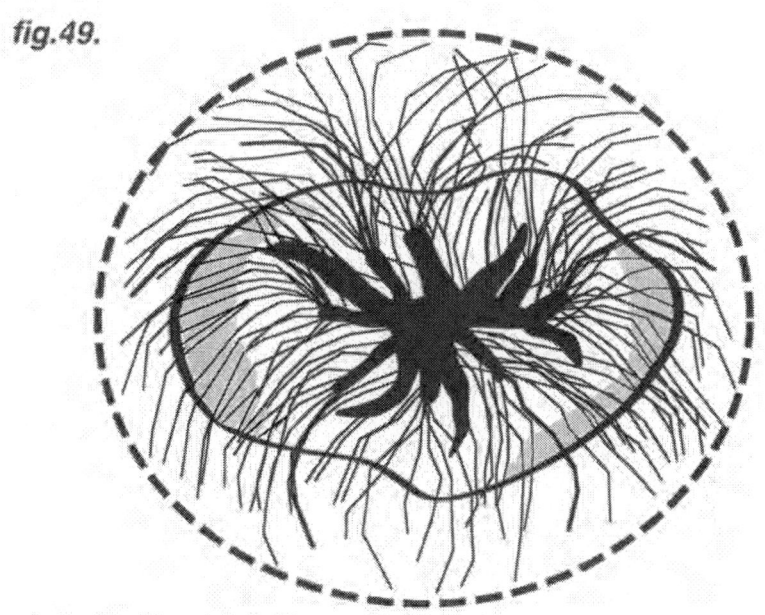

fig.49.

When viewed from above, the tree should have a rounded shape.

I have always found it very helpful in creating my tree sculpture, to look at and study the structure of trees. The variety is almost endless. The next time you are looking at trees, note the relationship and proportion between the height of the trunk compared to the roots and the branches. Look closely at the branches and twigs and observe the interesting and sometimes strange shapes, twists and angular bends they form. You will also notice that in almost all trees there is tapering of the branches as they grow out from the trunk.

The Weeping Willow

This is the final look of the Weeping Willow tree sculpture. If your tree does not appear as this one, or does not have the look you want, you can very easily un-bend the wire branches and try again. Wire is very resilent and can be bent and unbent and formed into different shapes many times. You will find, as I did, that the more you work with the wire, the better you get at it. I have created the tree shown here on a flat piece of glass. If you like you can also create the tree in a small pot or container.

Creating The Beaded Tree Sculpture

THE BASIC BEADED TREE

The beaded tree sculpture is created by first making the Weeping Willow tree, as shown on page 36, then adding the beads to the twig end wires. Since the weeping willow tree is very easy to create, this tree is also easy to create.

BEAD VARIETIES

Although you can use any type of small bead that will slide onto the wire, the type of beads that I think look the best are called "Fringe Beads" They are so named because the hole in the bead is in the top part of the bead, not in the center as most beads.

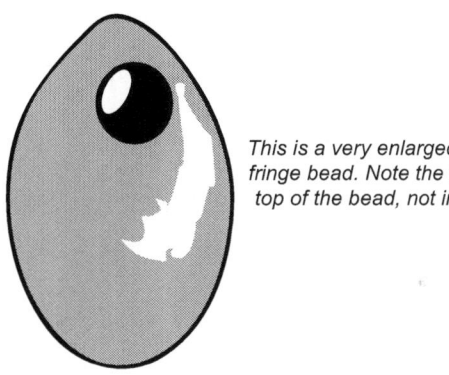

This is a very enlarged view of the fringe bead. Note the hole is at the top of the bead, not in the center.

I chose to use this type of bead because it hangs from the twigs, rather than having the twig pass through the bead. I feel this give the beads on the tree a more natural look. The fringe beads I use are made of glass. They are manufactured in a very wide variety of colors. And each color is offered in several different finishes, including: solid, rainbow, clear matte, and gunmetal. I like the "clear rainbow" color because they catch and reflect the light very dramatically. When this type of bead is used and the tree sculpture is displayed in direct sunlight or a very bright light, the beads seem to glisten and glow. Even if you use the same color beads for the entire piece, the light will bounce and reflect off each bead at a different angle creating a kaleidoscope of color. And, since the beads are hanging loose from the wire, they are free to move slightly in a gentle breeze or the least vibration, adding more color and variation to the creation.

I will sometimes use all of one color beads for the entire tree or mix several colors together to get a specific effect. For example, I will use all clear beads on a tree made of sliver color wire mounted on a glass base. The combination of glass and silver gives the effect of a tree in a winter setting with ice clinging to its branches and snow covering the ground. I have also created beaded trees using several different shades of green beads producing a summer tree in full bloom.

If you wish you can also use beads that are named "Seed Beads" These are beads that have the holes in the center of the bead, not on the edge like the fringe beads. Seed beads also are available in a very large variety of colors and shapes. Please be sure that no matter what type of bead you are using, be sure the hole in the bead is large enough to accommodate the wire gauge you are using.

THE WIRE

Any type or color wire can be used with the fringe beads. The only restriction is the size (gauge) of the wire. Remember, the thickness or gauge of wire is given in numbers. However, THE SMALLER THE NUMBER, THE THICKER THE WIRE. For example, 24 gauge is thicker than 26 gauge. The best thickness of wire to use is 26 gauge for the tree sculpture shown here. 24 gauge can also be used but it is not as easy to work with. The fringe beads will not even fit on any wire larger than 24 gauge. Of course, if you wish you can use a thinner gauge wire or larger beads.

SELECTION OF BEADS

Begin by selecting the type of beads and colors you wish to use. If you choose to use a variety of colored beads on the same tree, mix all the colors before you start. Do not try to mix them as you go along. I usually mix all the different colored beads in a saucer or other wide flat dish. This makes it much easier to randomly pick up one bead at a time. Do not try to add the beads onto the tree in any set pattern or order. Doing so will create an uninteresting use of color and as in nature, the best creations are usually random. Do not be concerned if you find that as you are adding beads to the tree you have several beads of the same color all next to each other. This will actually look very nice when all the beads are in place. The number of beads needed for your tree will of course depend on the size of the tree and how closely you space the beads. The fringe beads are usually sold in small plastic bags of one hundred beads per bag. The fringe beads are inexpensive, I would suggest you place your first order of five hundred to one thousand. If after you finish your beaded tree sculpture, and you have extra beads you would like to use, you can glue the beads onto the base, giving the appearance of falling leaves or fruit.

ADDING THE BEADS TO THE TREE SCULPTURE

1. Start by opening the twig ends to create a "V" shape. This is where you will slide each bead onto the wire.

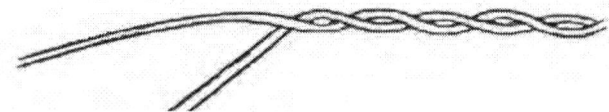

2. Slide one fringe bead onto the single wires. Move the bead to the double twisted wires.

3. Hold the bead in place tight against the double twisted wire using your thumb and index finger. Then, twist one end of the single wire over the top of the other single wire. Now, twist the wire an additional three to five times. This will lock the bead in place and create the necessary space to add the next bead.

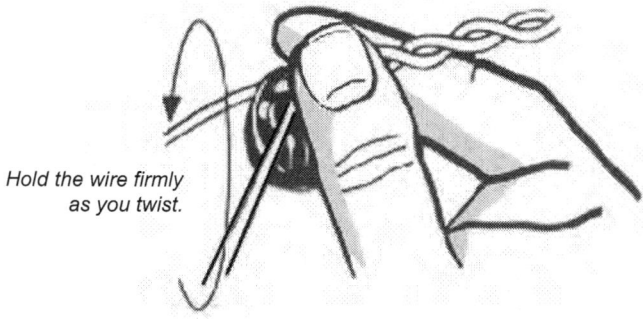

Hold the wire firmly as you twist.

4. All the remaining beads are added to the remaining twigs in the same way. Some twigs will have more or less than others. But each twig should have at least 2 beads.

5. As you add beads toward the end of the twig, try to leave enough wire after the last bead on the branch so you can create a small "V". This will give the twigs a very nice effect.

6. After all the beads have been added to all the twigs, shape the tree as explained on page 39. If you find you have a single strand of wire without a second wire on which to add a bead, just trim the single wire smaller and it will look like a twig.

The photo below is the final look for the Beaded Weeping Willow. If you feel your tree sculpture does not look like the one shown, you can easily unbend the wire and try again. The wire is very resilient and may be bent, shaped and re-worked many times, You will also find, as I did, the more you work with the wire the better you get at it.

The Beaded Weeping Willow

Creating The Wind Swept

Of all the styles of tree sculpture I have ever created, the Wind Swept receives the most comments and interest. Perhaps people like the movement they see in it, or maybe they can relate to the tenacity of the tree holding fast to the earth against the force of a mighty wind.

a)
Hold the tree firmly by the trunk. This is the best way to hold the piece securely as you work on the branches. This grip will also allow you to turn the tree and view it from different angles to be sure you are creating the shape you want.

b)
Spread out all the branches and twigs so they look like a fan. *fig. 50.* This fanning will make the tree appear flat, however we will create the roundness and fullness later on.

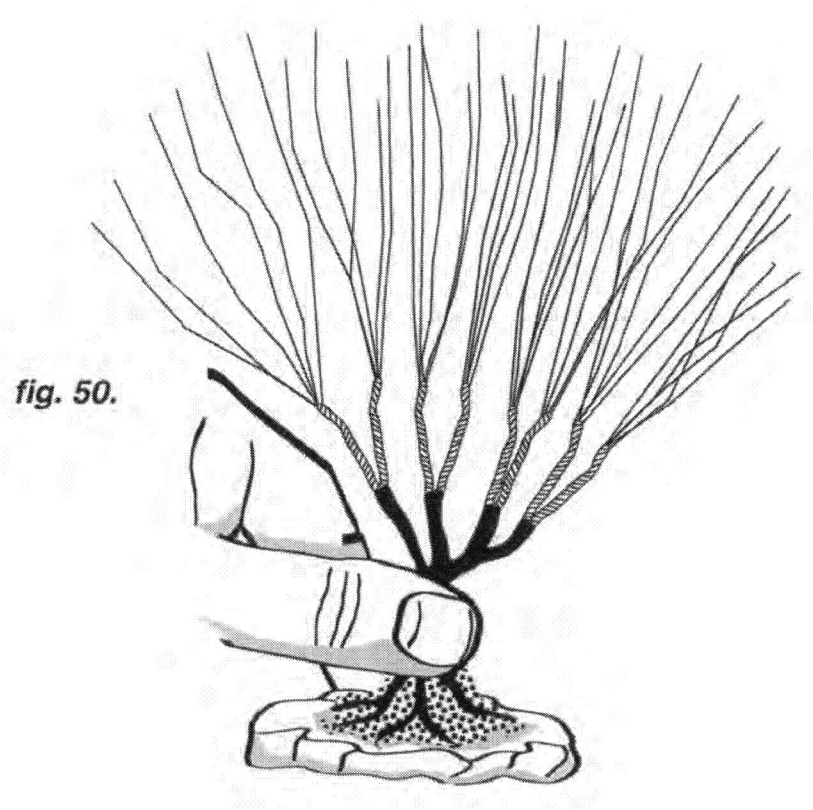

fig. 50.

c)

Hold the tree firmly at the top section of the trunk with one hand. With your other hand grip any two outermost branches at their "V" section. Twist the branches toward you 1/2 turn. **fig. 51.** This action will result in the two branches you have twisted becoming perpendicular to the branches next to them. Repeat this same function to every other set of two branches. The tree will now start to have a more rounded and full appearance.

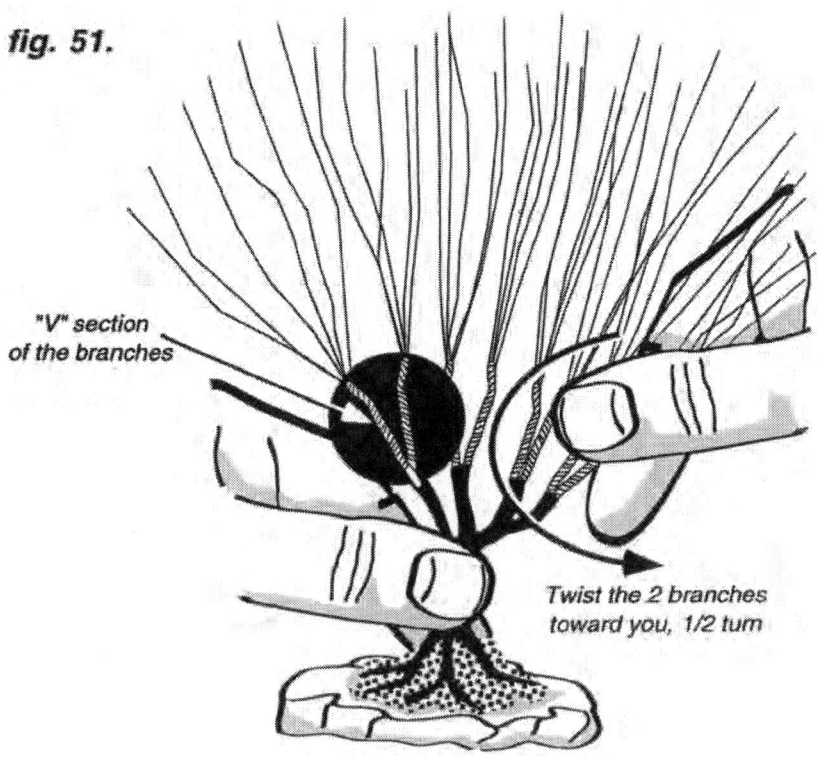

fig. 51.

"V" section of the branches

Twist the 2 branches toward you, 1/2 turn

d)
You are now going to work on the trunk of the tree sculpture to give it the wind swept look. Bending the trunk will add another element of resistance of the tree. This time hold the base of the sculpture in one hand and place the thumb of your other hand about half way up the trunk. Slowly bend the top half of the trunk over the top of your thumb as if you were trying to bend the tree in half. Continue bending the top half of the trunk until it appears to be about half way down the distance toward the roots. Do not be concerned about the trunk snapping, it is very flexible and can be easily formed into this position. *fig. 52.*

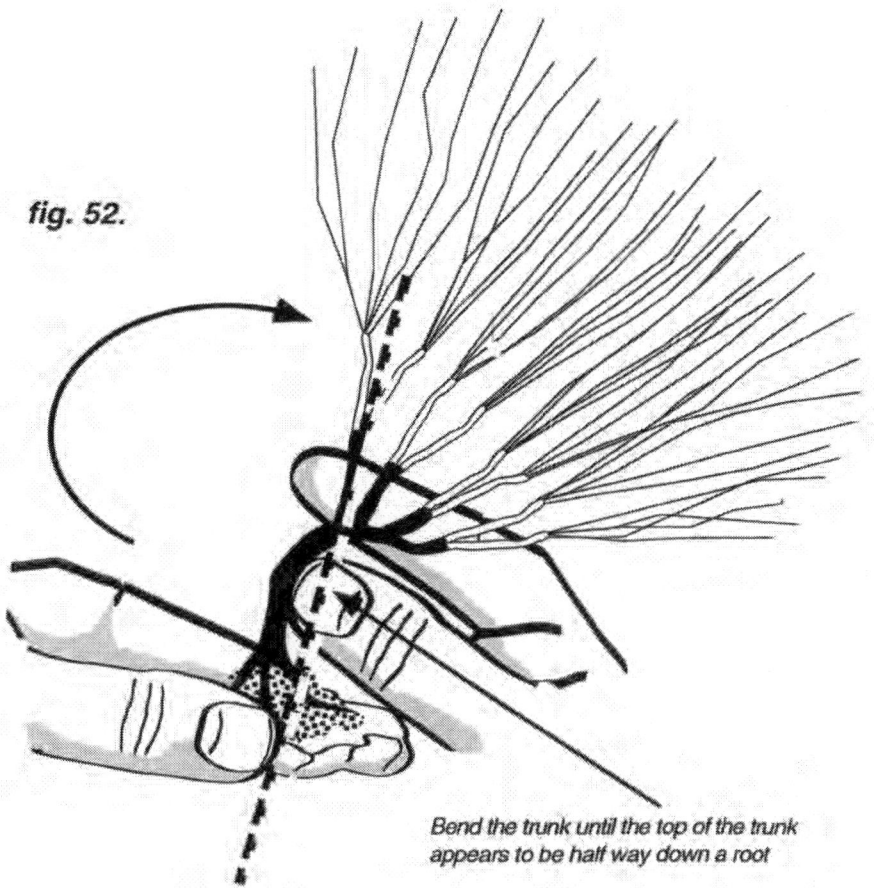

fig. 52.

Bend the trunk until the top of the trunk appears to be half way down a root

e)
Hold the tree firmly at the top of the trunk and bend a group of the branches in the opposite direction from which the trunk is bent. **fig.53.** Do not try to bend too many branches at one time. This opposite bending action is the action that will give the tree the appearance of bending, yet resisting the force of the wind. As you bend the branches also separate any branches that appear to be too close together. Move some of the branches down and some of the branches up. For the most part the branches should all be almost parallel to each other yet not exactly parallel. After all the bending is completed, if you feel any of the branches are too long you can either bend them into an "S" shape to use up some of the length of the wire or you can simply trim them using the small wire cutters.

fig. 53

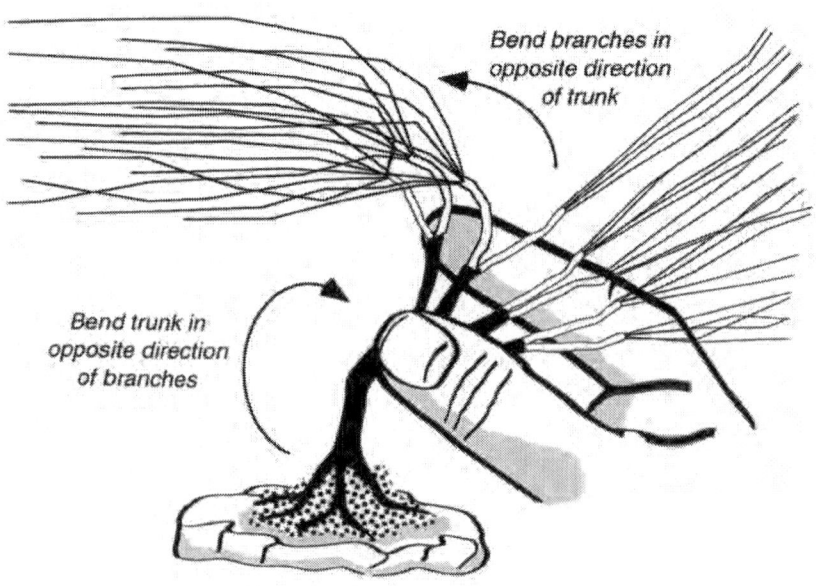

f)
As you are bending the branches, stop for a moment to look at the tree from directly above. *fig. 54.* The tree when viewed from this angle should have an oval and elongated shape. If you tree looks flat, pull the branches away from each other to create this elongated shape.

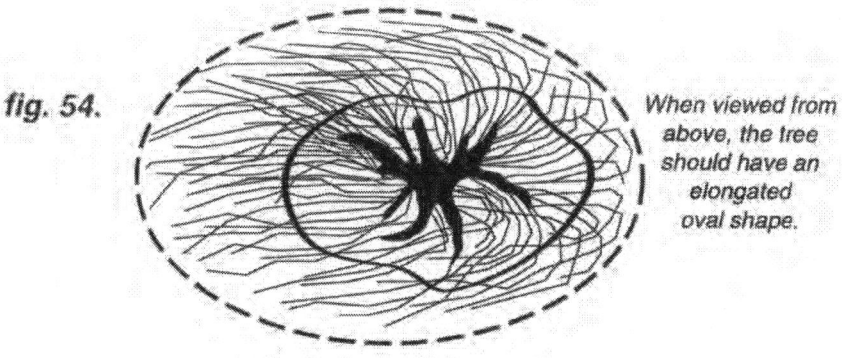

fig. 54.

When viewed from above, the tree should have an elongated oval shape.

The Wind Swept

Creating The Oak Tree

The Oak tree is more difficult to create than the other trees shown in this book. This tree will require more work on the creation of the branches and twigs. It will also involve some cutting of the longer twigs. This is also the basic form of the tree structure that will be used to create the "Bonsai with Leaves" (see page 60)

a)
Hold the tree firmly by the trunk. Once again, this is the best way to grip the tree as you work on it.

b)
Spread out all the branches so they look like a fan. All the branches and twigs should be on the same plane. The tree may look flat now, but we will shape it later on.

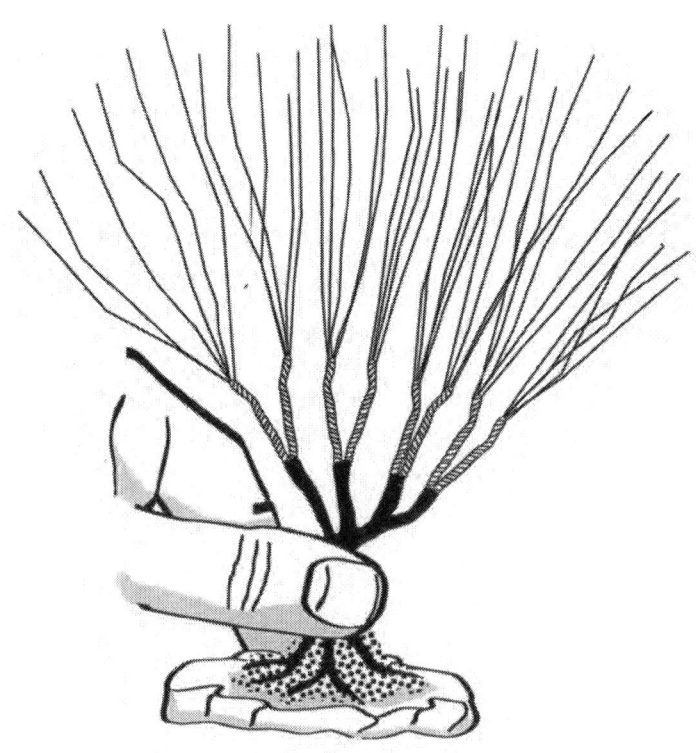

c)
The following steps illustrate how to create more different size branches and twigs for this tree. The look of the oak tree requires a varied amount and size of the branches and twigs. I think you will understand the procedures better after starting the sculpture. In the following steps you will be cutting the wires to create the branches and twigs. So, it is important that you are sure of the cut you are making before you make the cut. If after reading all the steps necessary to create the oak tree you feel you may have some difficulty creating the branches and twigs, I would suggest using some scrap wire to practice. Simply twist two pieces of wire together to create a practice branch.

d)
Gripping any outer branch at its base closest to the trunk, loop one single wire over the wire next to it to create an oval. ***fig. 56.*** The oval size should be about the circumference of your index finger. This first oval should be created about 1/4" to 3/8" from the thicker part of the branch closest to the trunk.

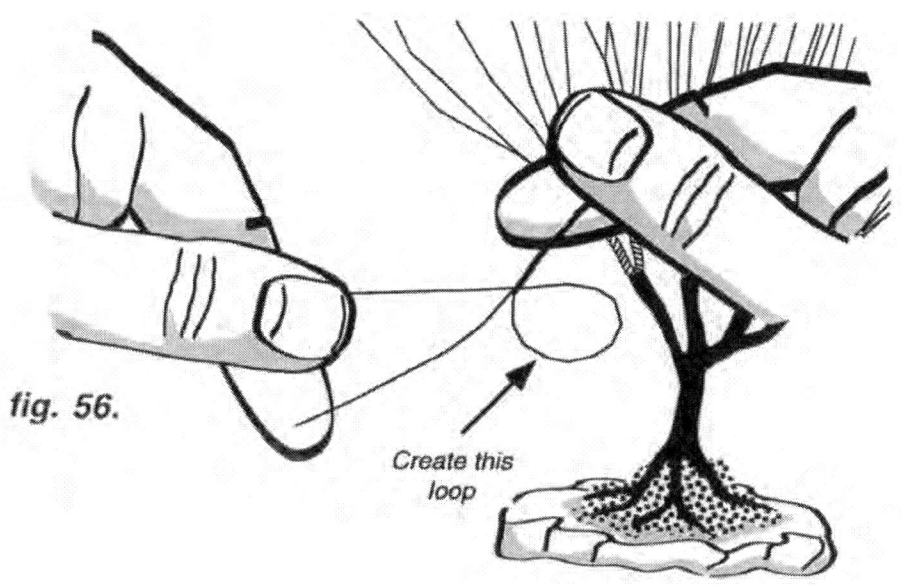

fig. 56.

Create this loop

e)
Hold the loop you just created and the other loose wires firmly and twist them in the opposite direction about four or five complete twists. If you like, you can perform each twisting action separately. *fig. 57.*

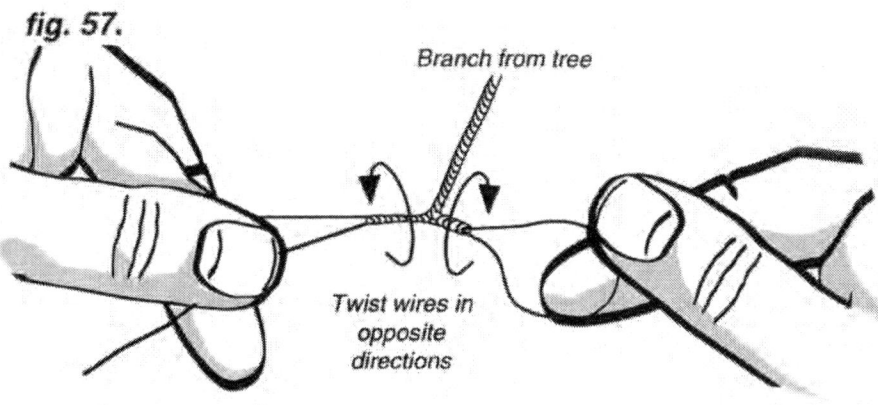

fig. 57.

f)
Repeat step e). In each step use the longer section of the loose wires to create the next loop. Continue repeating step e) to create as many loops you can with the section of wire. *fig. 58.* You should be able to create two to four loops per pair of wires. Do not be concerned if the loops you created are different sizes, this will actually add more interest to the piece.

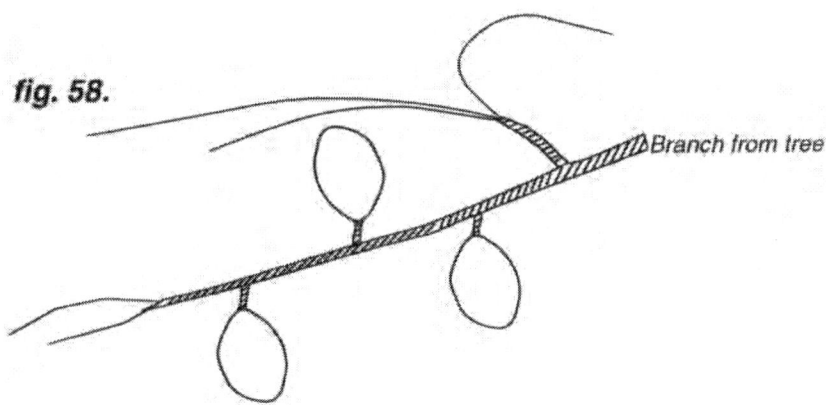

fig. 58.

g)
Use the preceding steps on all the remaining pairs of wires on the tree. Should you come across a branch with an extra wire that you cannot pair with another, just leave it as a single wire. All extra wires will be trimmed in the following steps.

h)
After you have created all the loops on the tree, you are now ready to cut the loops to create the final smallest twigs. (If you are going to create the beaded tree, these small twigs are where you will be adding the beads.) Use the small wire cutters for this step. I have learned through experience, the safest way to cut any wire. Whenever you make a cut in the wire, try to keep the cut perpendicular to the wire. *fig. 59.* This cutting will create blunter ends in the wire rather than "knife blades". This procedure will not eliminate all cuts, but should lessen them. I have also found it is much better to work slow when handling the cut ends of wire. I have also tried working with gloves on but I find it too restricting. However, if you find you can work in gloves you should do it!

fig. 59.

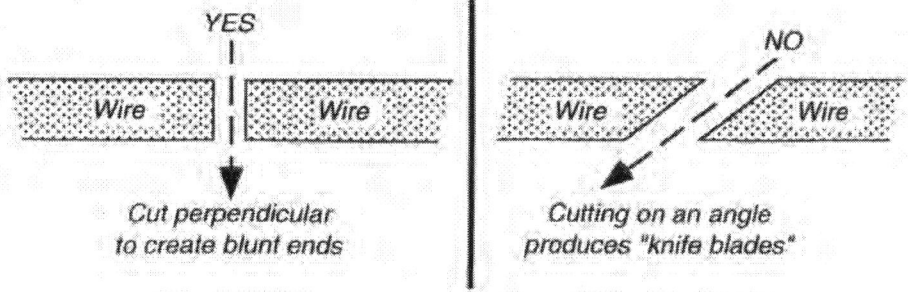

i)

Cut each loop once. This will create two twigs growing from a the branch. Do not cut the loops exactly in the center. Cut each loop in a slightly different location to create twigs that are of varied sizes. After you cut the loop and create the twigs, grip the end of each twig and gently pull on it so it is more straightened. The goal here is to remove most of the round shape from each twig and make it more angular and not as even. If any of the end wires are too long, now is the time to trim them. ***fig. 60.***

fig. 60.

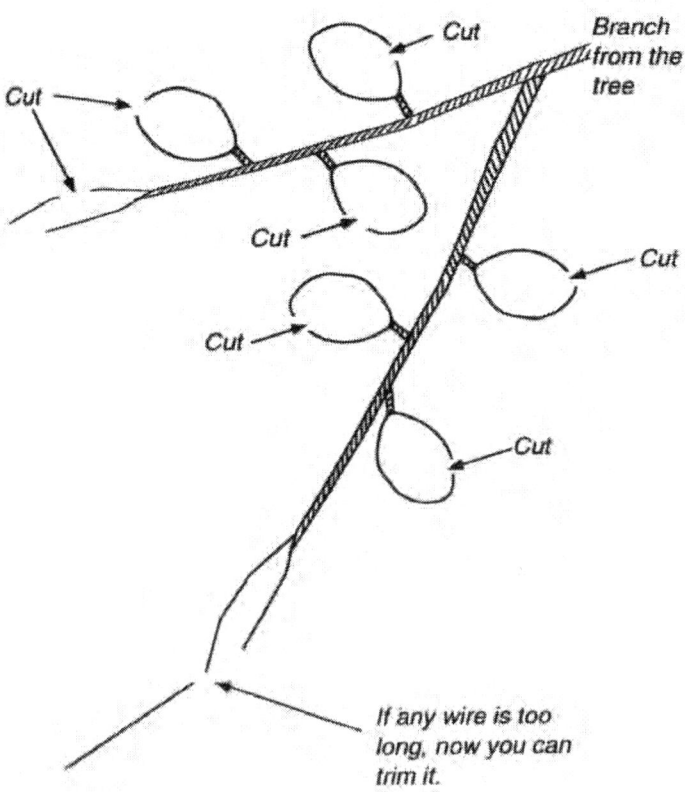

j)
We are now at the point where you will make all the wire look like an actual oak tree. This next section is perhaps the most artistically difficult part, but it is also the most rewarding. Upon completion of the following steps, if you do not like the resulting look of your tree sculpture, you can very easily repeat the final steps. The wire you are working with is very workable and can be bent and re-shaped many times. *fig. 61.*

k)
Push all the branches and twigs straight up, and flatten the sections that are closest to the top of the trunk. Now spread out and separate the main branches.

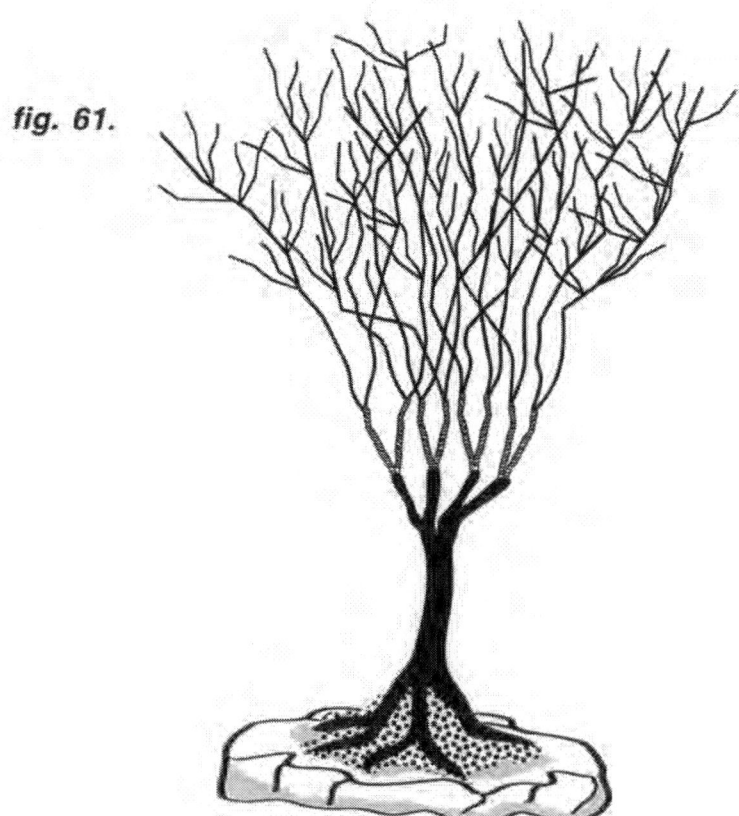

fig. 61.

l)

You are now ready to begin to style and shape the outermost twigs of the tree. *fig. 62.* If you have ever looked closely at the twigs of an oak tree, or almost any tree, you will have noticed that the twigs seem to go in every conceivable direction with no particular rhyme or reason. The twigs are never evenly spaced nor are they bunched together. I was told by a friend, who is a science teacher, that this random spacing is due to the efforts of the leaves on the tree to receive as much sunlight as possible. The structure and position of the twigs is much more noticeable in the winter when there are no leaves on the tree.

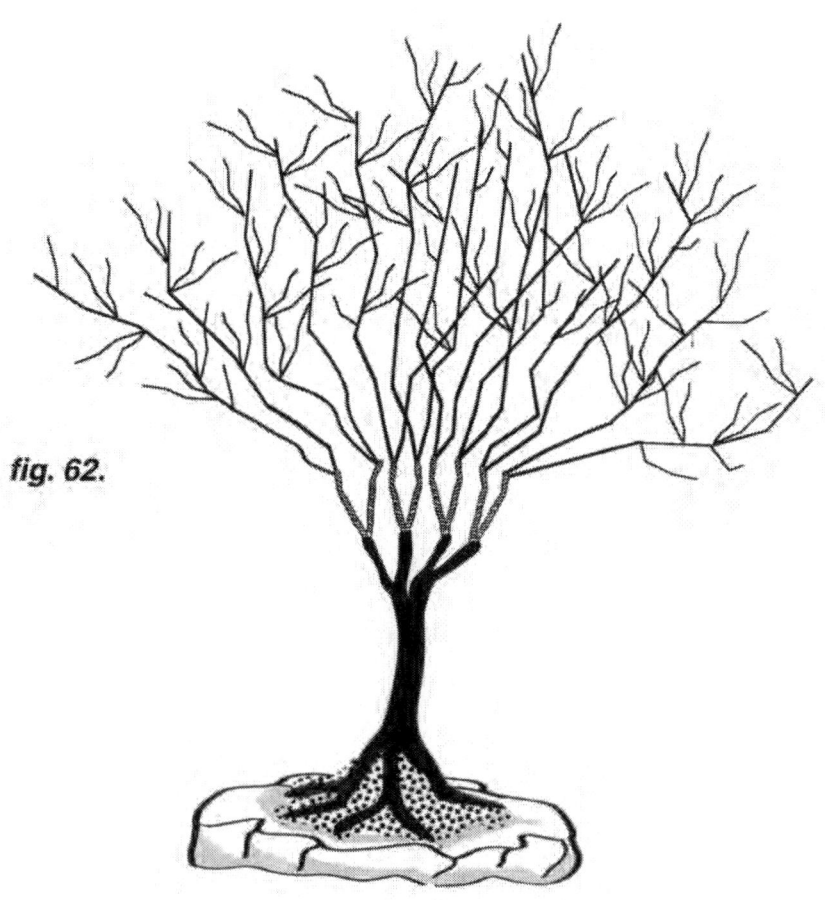

fig. 62.

The characteristic of the wire you are using lends itself very effetely to capturing the structure of the twigs. The wire will hold its shape once you bend it into the position you want. Fan out and separate all the twigs so that no two twigs are touching. After this procedure you tree should look like an open fan.

m)
Hold the tree from the top section of the trunk and bend each of the branches in the opposite direction of the branch next to it. You will notice that this action will start to create a more rounded and full appearance of the tree. *fig. 63.*

fig. 63.

n)
As you are bending the twigs, stop for a moment to look at the tree from directly above. *fig. 64.* The tree when viewed from this angle should have a round shape. If your tree looks flat, pull the branches away from each other to create the necessary roundness.

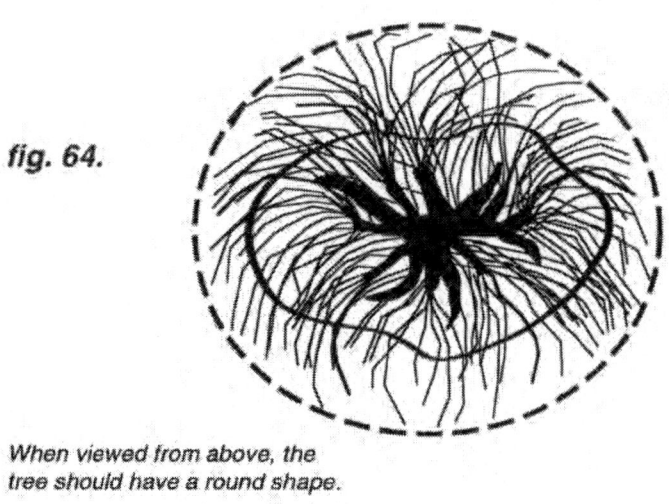

fig. 64.

When viewed from above, the tree should have a round shape.

o)
As a final step to create more variety in the shape of the twigs, bend every third twig at a ninety degree angle at about the half way point of the twig. This will create more of the bends, twists and turns we are looking for. *fig. 65.*

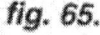

fig. 65.

The Oak Tree

Bonsai With Leaves

The tools you will need to create the leaves for the Bonsai with Leaves are:

1) A ball peen hammer. (if you don't have this type of hammer, a small regular hammer will do).

2) A jewelers anvil or, the flat side of a large hammer, or a solid piece of steel that is at least 1/2" thick by 5" x 4".

Since you will be working metal to metal you must use a hard metal surface to work on. Do not work on wood, or cement, or a rock. Be sure you always use eye protection!

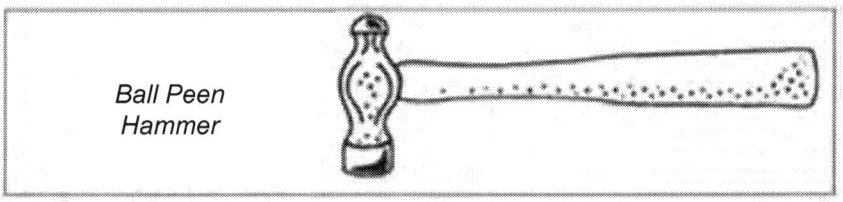

Ball Peen Hammer

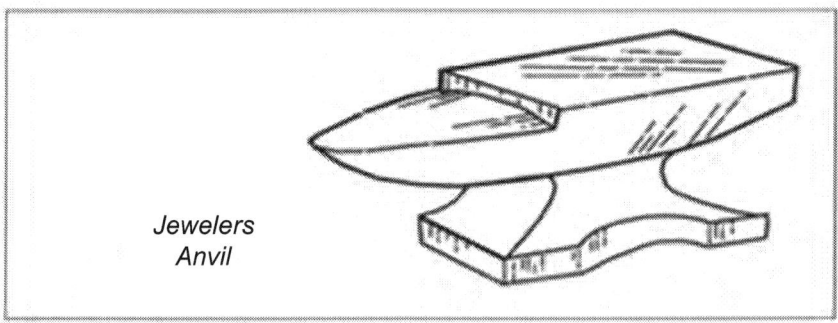

Jewelers Anvil

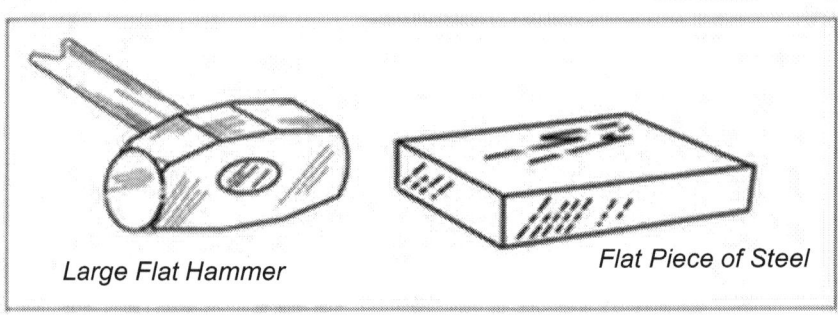

Large Flat Hammer

Flat Piece of Steel

The Bonsai with Leaves tree sculpture is created by the same techniques and instructions used to create the Oak tree.

Start by following all the steps on page **50** through **55** ending with step **k) fig. 61.** on page **55**.

Once you have created the Oak tree you will be ready to change the end of the twigs into flat leaves.

a)
Hold the tree firmly by the trunk and spread out the branches one at a time so it looks like a opened fan. Try to keep the twigs on a flat plane. Bend any twigs out of the way so you will be able to hammer the twigs one at a time. This will make it easier to hammer the ends of the twigs when you place them on the metal hammering surface.

b)
You are now ready to start creating the leaves. I think it is a very good idea to practice creating the leaves using some scrap wire before you actually start on the leaves of the tree.

c)
Hold the trunk firmly and place the end of one twig on the hammering surface. Hammer the end of the twig no more than 4 or 5 times until it is flat. The leaf you create should be about 1/2" long. Do not over hammer the leaf, this will weaken the stem which holds the leaf to the branch. Do not try to make all the leaves look alike. It is better if they don't.

d)
Repeat step **c)** to create all the remaining leaves.

e)
Creating leaves on a small tree made of thin wire requires patience and care. Be extra careful after you have created all the leaves. Try not to over bend the leaf at the place where it meets the branch, this is the weakest point of the leaf structure. You will find that no matter how careful you are some of the leaves will be broken and fall off. Simply leave the remaining twig as is, do not try to re-hammer the remaining part of the twig. You will simply cause more of the leaves to fall off if you do. For the best results - take your time!

f)
You are now ready to shape the tree. Hold the tree firmly from the top part of the trunk. Twist each of the branches in the opposite direction of the branch next to it. This action will give the tree a rounded shape and a more natural look.

g)
As you carefully bend the branches as instructed, stop from time to time and look at the tree from directly above it. The tree should have a round or oval shape. If you feel your tree looks flat, pull some of the branches away from each other, this will create a more rounded shape

h)

For the final shaping step I like to bend all or most of the leaves so that they are pointing downward. This gives the leaves a more realistic look and will allow the leaves to catch and reflect the light at different angles. For more variety I bend some leaves entirely down, for some I bend the leaf at its half way point. I also keep some of the leaves flat then give them a slight twist. This twisting will give the leaf a softer look. Be very careful when you are bending the leaves. You can, if you choose, keep all or most of the leaves flat and not bent. Exactly as they look after you first hammered them.

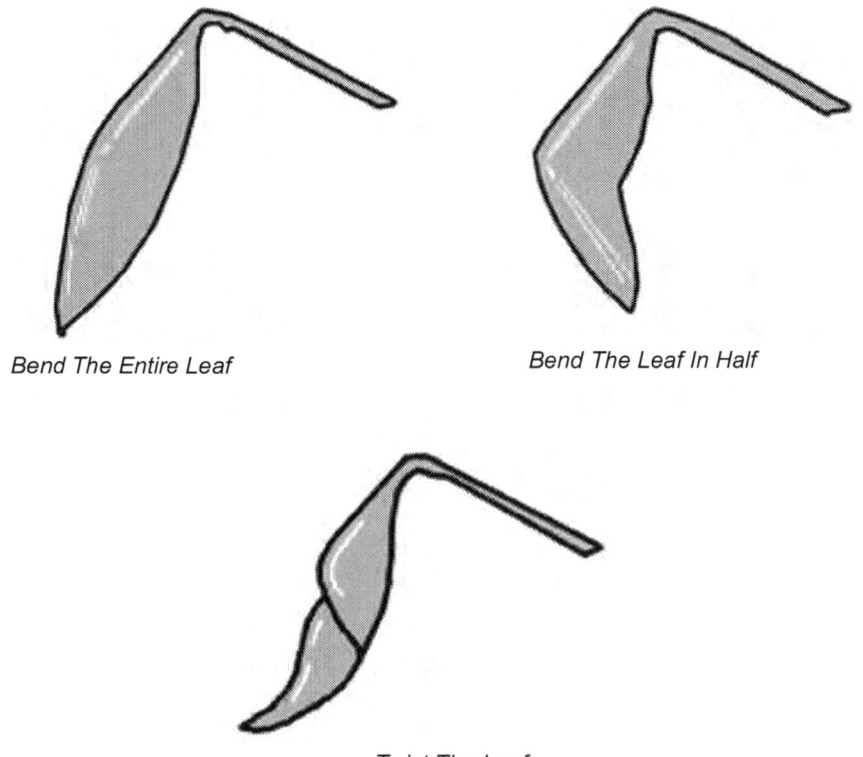

Bend The Entire Leaf   *Bend The Leaf In Half*

Twist The Leaf

Bonsai With Leaves

You have now completed all the necessary steps and procedures to create a tree sculpture. I hope you are happy with the results. I have tried to make the steps as simple and clear as possible. If you wish to create other tree sculpture of different sizes and shapes you can use these instructions and tools as your basic guide. I would suggest that you try different ways to make your tree sculpture, and also try to use different gauge and types of wire. Most of what I have learned about creating tree sculpture and working with the wire has come from trial and error. (Sometimes more error than I like to admit). I have always tried to learn from the piece I am working on, the things to do, and not to do on the next piece.

If you would like to see more of my tree sculptures, please visit my web site, and once again, I hope you are happy with your tree sculpture creation.

I would be happy to hear from you with any comments or suggestions about my work. You can contact me at:

Sal Villano
PO Box 827
Milford, Ohio 45150

email: salvillano@gmail.com

web site: www.salvillano.com

Thank You!

About The Artist

Sal Villano was born in New York City in 1944 into a large extended family of many artists. So, he was always very aware of art in his life and was naturally attracted to expressing himself visually. He attended public grade school, high school and college. He also studied at The Art Students League in Manhattan. While still in college he assisted his uncle Charles Santaniello, a sculptor, in creating commercial displays for many New York businesses. And helped produce parts of an exhibit for a Worlds Fair in Europe.

It was this time spent working with his uncle that he realized he too wanted to be a sculptor. After graduating college he went to work as a commercial artist. In 1969, after several years at this position he started his own art studio with another artist, this partnership provided the opportunity to produce a wide verity of commercial work both two dimensional and three dimensional.

It was at the time he spent at the Art Students league that Sal created his first wire tree sculpture, While constructing an armature to support a clay figure, he noticed that the wire he was using could also be bent, twisted and wrapped to create a tree sculpture. Since that day, many years ago, he has created thousands of tree sculptures of various wire types and gauges and each carefully placed onto a base that is a vital part of the total piece.

Whether viewed in direct sunlight casting harsh shadows or in soft candle light creating a gentle form, the tree sculptures created by Sal Villano each take on a personality of their own. As in nature, no two trees can ever be created alike.

All the sculpture of Sal Villano can be viewed at:
www.salvillano.com

TOOLS NEEDED

- Small Hammer
- 1/2" Soft Brush
- No.1 or 0 Art Brush
- Small Wire Cutters
- Medium Wire Cutters
- Jewelers Anvil -OR- Large Flat Hammer -OR- Flat Piece of Steel at least 1/2" x 5" x 4"

MATERIAL NEEDED

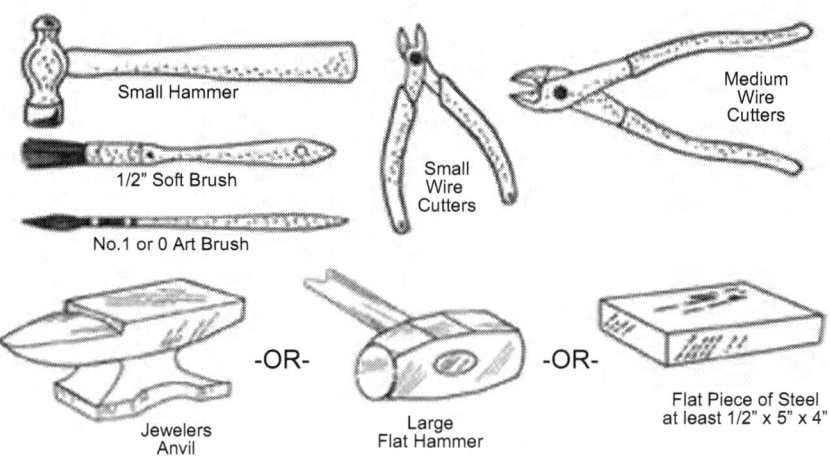

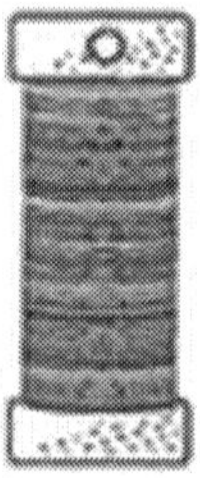

At least 1 spool of wire (about 1/4 lb.) The wire should be 26 or 28 gauge. Can be any color.

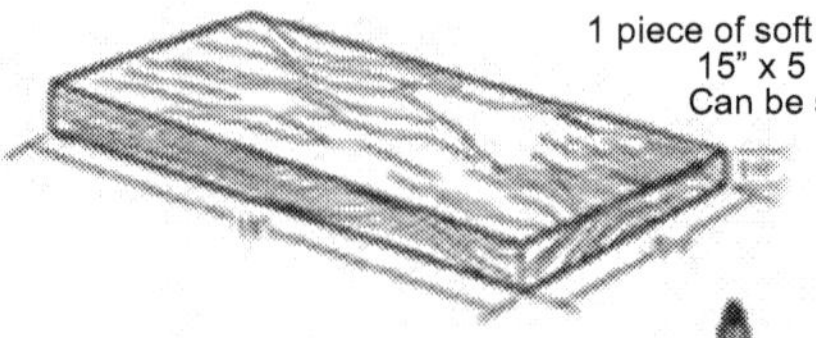

1 piece of soft wood about 15" x 5 1/2" x 1 1/2" Can be scrap wood.

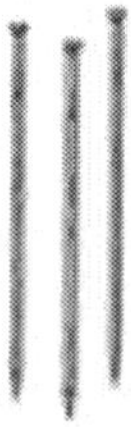

Base material for tree. About 2 1/2" x 1 1/2" This can be glass, rock or any other item that will bond with the white glue.

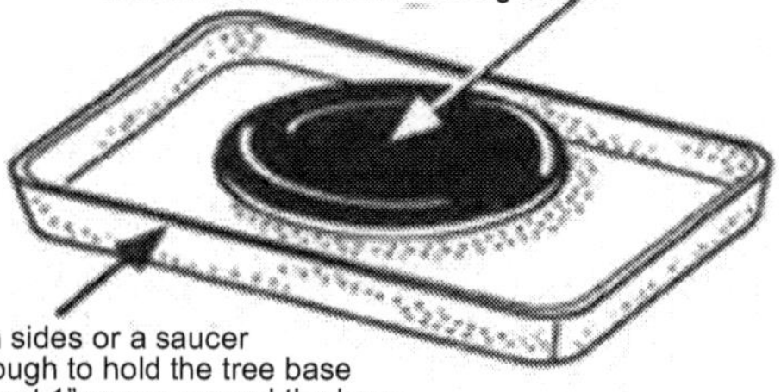

Three, 2 1/2" finishing nails

Small bottles of Yellow, Green and White India Ink.

Tray with sides or a saucer large enough to hold the tree base with at least 1" space around the base

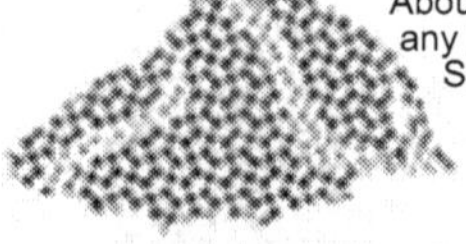

About 2 cups of beach sand or any type of sand you choose. Sand can contain small pebbles or other natural material.

Masking Tape

Small bottle of White Glue with applicator point on top. Be sure the glue will bond onto the base material and with the sand mixture.

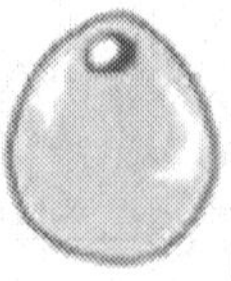

Fringe Beads (for the beaded tree sculpture only)

This is an enlarged view. Note the hole is at the top of the bead.

Printed in Great Britain
by Amazon.co.uk, Ltd.,
Marston Gate.